Carl Schmitt and the Intensification of Politics

MODERNITY AND POLITICAL THOUGHT

Series Editors
Morton Schoolman
State University of New York at Albany
and
Kennan Ferguson
University of South Florida

This unique collection of original studies of the great figures in the history of political and social thought critically examines their contributions to our understanding of modernity, its constitution, and the promise and problems latent within it. These works are written by some of the finest theorists of our time for scholars and students of the social sciences and humanities.

The Augustine Imperative: A Reflection on the Politics of Morality
    by *William E. Connolly*
Emerson and Self-Reliance
    by *George Kateb*
Edmund Burke: Modernity, Politics, and Aesthetics
    by *Stephen K. White*
Jean-Jacques Rousseau: The Politics of the Ordinary
    by *Tracy B. Strong*
Michel Foucault and the Politics of Freedom
    by *Thomas L. Dumm*
Reading "Adam Smith": Desire, History, and Value
    by *Michael J. Shapiro*
Thomas Hobbes: Skepticism, Individuality, and Chastened Politics
    by *Richard E. Flathman*
Thoreau's Nature: Ethics, Politics, and the Wild
    by *Jane Bennett*
G. W. F. Hegel: Modernity and Politics
    by *Fred R. Dallmayr*
The Reluctant Modernism of Hannah Arendt
    by *Seyla Benhabib*
Aquinas and Modernity: The Lost Promise of Natural Law
    by *Shadia Drury*
Merleau-Ponty and Modern Politics after Anti-Humanism
    by *Diana Coole*
William James: Politics in the Pluriverse
    by *Kennan Ferguson*
Carl Schmitt and the Intensification of Politics
    by *Kam Shapiro*

Carl Schmitt and the Intensification of Politics

Kam Shapiro

ROWMAN & LITTLEFIELD PUBLISHERS, INC.
Lanham • Boulder • New York • Toronto • Plymouth, UK

ROWMAN & LITTLEFIELD PUBLISHERS, INC.

Published in the United States of America
by Rowman & Littlefield Publishers, Inc.
A wholly owned subsidary of The Rowman & Littlefield Publishing Group, Inc.
4501 Forbes Boulevard, Suite 200, Lanham, Maryland 20706
www.rowmanlittlefield.com

Estover Road
Plymouth PL6 7PY
United Kingdom

Copyright © 2008 by Rowman & Littlefield Publishers, Inc.
First paperback edition 2010

British Library Cataloguing in Publication Information Available

Library of Congress Cataloging-in-Publication Data
Shapiro, Kam.
   Carl Schmitt and the intensification of politics / J. Kam Shapiro.
      p. cm. — (Modernity and political thought)
   Includes bibliographical references and index.
   1. Schmitt, Carl, 1888–1985. 2. Democracy. 3. Sovereignty. 4. Globalization.
   5. International relations. I. Title.
JC263.S34S53 2008
321.8—dc22   2008003878

   ISBN: 978-0-7425-3342-4 (pbk. alk. paper)

Printed in the United States of America

⊗ ™ The paper used in this publication meets the minimum requirements of
American National Standard for Information Sciences—Permanence of Paper
for Printed Library Materials, ANSI/NISO Z39.48-1992.

~

Contents

	Series Editors' Introduction	vii
	Preface	xvii
	Acknowledgments	xix
Chapter 1	Schmitt at Large	1
Chapter 2	Channels of Political Authority	17
Chapter 3	From Ethos to Pathos	37
Chapter 4	Globalization and Nihilism	67
Chapter 5	Carl Schmitt and the Intensification of Politics	97
	Bibliography	121
	Index	127
	About the Author	131

~

Series Editors' Introduction

J. Kam Shapiro's *Carl Schmitt and the Intensification of Politics* is volume 14 of *Modernity and Political Thought*, the Rowman & Littlefield series in contemporary political theory. Shapiro's work follows publication of Shadia Drury's *Aquinas and Modernity: The Lost Promise of Natural Law*, Diana Coole's *Merleau-Ponty and Modern Politics after Anti-Humanism*, and Kennan Ferguson's *William James: Politics in the Pluriverse*[1] (volumes 13, 12, and 11, respectively), and new editions of the original ten volumes in the series.[2] Initially designed to include only ten volumes, *Modernity and Political Thought* has been expanded to include, in addition to the works by Shapiro, Drury, Coole, and Ferguson, forthcoming studies of Karl Marx by Wendy Brown, Aristotle by Mary Dietz, Thomas More by Peter Euben, Publius by Jason Frank, Sigmund Freud by James Glass, J. S. Mill by Kirstie McClure, John Rawls by Donald Moon, Friedrich Nietzsche by David Owen, David Hume by Davide Panagia, William Connolly by Kathleen Skerrett, Niccolo Machiavelli by Miguel Vatter, and Sheldon Wolin by Nicholas Xenos. Moreover, we expect this list to grow in the future. As those who are familiar with these authors' previous works will expect, their forthcoming studies adopt a variety of approaches and pose diverse and creative questions about these figures in political theory. Contributors to *Modernity and Political Thought* critically examine ways in which major political theorists shape our understanding of modernity—not only its origins and constitution but also its overt and latent problems, promises, and dangers.

In his earlier study, *Sovereign Nations, Carnal States*, Shapiro originally came to Schmitt by way of the body.[3] Schmitt's politics, he holds, are grounded in a profound understanding of a people's affective intensities and energies, all ideally manifest in a central national-political authority. As Shapiro demonstrates in this earlier work, Schmitt did not arrive at this realization alone, but was influenced by Georges Sorel, by Eduard Spranger, and—most importantly—by G. F. W. Hegel. Nor, Shapiro argues, was Schmitt's ideal the only possible use of these affective intensities, as Walter Benjamin's similar but potentially redemptive and antifascist politicizations show.

How these divergent interpretations emerge from attention to what Shapiro identifies as "somatics" takes some explanation. Hegel, Schmitt, and Benjamin all recognize the importance of bodily practices of habit, emotion, and capacity. To take the body seriously, in Shapiro's words, as a site of "an intersection of forces and thresholds of organization where the confluence of the material and the intelligible is negotiated," (12–13) as do each of these authors, means to focus on situated processes involving intellect, will, and corporeality. All avoid the common pitfalls of thinking of bodies as somehow prehuman (the unchanging biological ground from which an isolated humanity emerges) or, conversely, merely a social formation (an effect of ideology or some other, more "real" systematization).

They are not alone here, and Shapiro describes a triumvirate of other, more overtly somatically oriented, theorists to clarify the methods and stakes: Augustine, Nietzsche, and Derrida. Each of these authors hearkens to somatic practices as both disciplinary and world-creating. Each recognizes the appetites and demands of the body as *excess*, as realms of experience irreducible to meaning, faith, and intellect, and as *subtending*, as both supporting and undermining connections, identities, and localities. In the face of this realization, each also suggests methods and traditions used to shape and intensify the body's energies and capacities. Bodies, the three argue, site and localize values and modes of being, and because they do so quite overtly they provide the springboard for Shapiro's discussion of a more complex somatics.

Augustine, for example, famously decried carnal desire. Even when the soul desired purity, the body would repeatedly pull it toward sin—this, he argued, was the message of the Fall. But, Shapiro notes, Augustine's solution is not simply to privilege the soul over the body, but instead to train the body to resist temptation. Once so trained, Augustine promises, the body can become habituated to the good. Yet this process is not easy—habits are difficult to develop, those of the body deeply rooted. Thus the will needs to be ever-conscious of the possibility of the separation from God. Confession, for Augustine, serves to set the willed, would-be habituation (leading to the desired communion with God) against the sensuous and habituated pulls of the body, with the cycle continually fed through the impossibility of resolution.

Nietzsche also suggests disciplines of the body, of thought, and of morals as the preconditions for their development. Unlike Augustine, Nietzsche sees the productive nature of such practices as open-ended—they need not operate according to a monotheistic god's clear instructions. Nor can disciplines be reduced to habits of denial, as they are assumed to be by Augustine. Invention, thematization, appropriation, and guesswork all comprise forms of training that develop the self. We re-create ourselves from these groundworks of practices, groundworks already woven within our bodies and our environs.

But Nietzsche's approach is more than merely an appreciation for affective life, wherein one pays attention to one's passions for example. Shapiro points out that habit "is already operant in affect" (39). What we like or dislike, what intrigues or repels, arises from our personal genealogies, histories already developed within and inscribed upon our bodies. The point is neither to reduce selfhood to the body, nor to free the intellect from it. Nietzsche's goal, instead, is to develop, repeat, multiply, and learn to control the varieties of affective potentiality available to all. In doing so, one opens up latent creativities both within the self and within the work of being; one becomes an artist rather than a consumer. Shapiro shows that this cannot be mere liberation or, conversely, mere moderation. Instead, it is a pluralization of "habits, of possible configurations of experience and action" (47). The appreciation for alterity within one's own experience can result in an appreciation for the alterity of others: their lives, their opinions, their cultures.

Intriguingly, Shapiro also includes Jacques Derrida as the third member of this somatic group. In the popular imagination Derrida remains firmly tied to deconstructive approaches to textuality (often misrepresented as an anything-goes approach to interpretation, wherein a work means anything the deconstructionist wants it to mean). In contrast, Shapiro finds in Derrida a careful and unending attention to the structural components of language and its conditions, situated irrevocably alongside the simultaneous understanding that utterances constantly play off against and exceed these conditions. For Derrida, an "organon of iterability"—the conditions under which the sayable is sayable—can never be disentangled from "ruptures of presence"—the transportation of those conditions into creative and unexpected contours. Language cannot exist without demarcations and delimitations, in other words, but neither do such forms predetermine its usages or potentialities.

Creative deployments of these kinds may seem restricted to language, but within the Derridian universe language and metaphysics operate together. The conditionalities of language (and the freedoms contained therein) are parallel to, or even constitutive of, the conditionalities of morality, ethics, and presence (and the freedoms contained therein as well). This has two important results. First, as in Nietzsche's work, such developments combine habit and ethics into an overarching framework of will and negotiation. Second, it explicitly recognizes the destructive and violent elements of all ethical and political decisions, actions, or utterances: each exists within and beyond the boundaries of morality, law, ontology, and epistemology.

Each of these preceding thinkers, Shapiro argues, responds to the demands made by the somatic passions. But from what historical conditions do our contemporary passions emerge? Shapiro identifies Hegel as tying these divergent strands of affect and tradition into an overarching political theory, one that relies upon *habit* at both the personal and the national level. For Hegel, to become habituated is not to remove individual willfulness, as might be supposed, but to negotiate its proper place in public, social space. Within the nation (as for any communal identity), purely individual will poses a problem. Being both subjective and particular, such will tends toward "the unmarshaled inclinations of the individual" (64). In order to operate politically, the will must therefore be subjected. But this subjection must depend upon a social and relational manner: the individual, for Hegel, emerges from the complex relationships between universalism and singularity.

Shapiro describes Hegel as undermining the simplistic notion that habituation can be divided from rationality, in part by rejecting the univocity of Cartesian mind-body dualism. Habit "appears out of the negation of domination of feeling by mind, which imposes itself on the body" (73) but this is not a one-way path, as "the autonomy of the intellect itself is grounded in and depends upon the organization—and thus containment—of feeling accomplished by habit" (74). Habits are thus *developed*—they can emerge from desires and goals, from attention as much as lack of attention. In fact, Hegel points out, life without habituation becomes meaningless, merely a set of fleeting and fragile connections. Only through the consolidation of the attachments of everyday life, the internalization of these contingencies, can we act freely. One must learn to drive an automobile, but not until the mechanics of driving are habituated can one negotiate driving's complex challenges or simultaneously engage in other behaviors or conversations. Habit is freeing.

Not until the body is properly habituated, then, can it truly become part of civil society. Shapiro attends particularly to Hegel's later writings, wherein society is seen as helping to inculcate the proper habits (under the term "education") for communal identity. The uneducated, unsocialized man remains particular, idiosyncratic, and unable to truly join with his fellow humans; the properly habituated man conceptualizes his actions and behaviors in terms of community, rank, and role. These habits are not universal, Shapiro reminds us, since they vary according to nation, class, and situation. Indeed, many organizational habituations may even overtly conflict with one another.

Thus the need for "police," a term that far exceeds the constabulary. For Hegel, Shapiro argues, policing includes all institutions established to control disruption and "regulate the contingency intrinsic to the complex interconnections of civil society" (87). This idea of the police as a transdisciplinary set of forces, with both regulative and productive power, will later influence the political theorizing of Foucault, Pasquino, and Rancière.[4] For Hegel, policing has an administrative side (that of the state), a regulative side (that of community), and a temperamental side (that of habit). The last one, no less than the first two, comprises a central recondition for the maintenance of order. What Hegel never develops, Shapiro points out, is a grand unified theory of policing that shows how these various administrations connect to and reinforce one another.

Carl Schmitt provides the specifics of such a theory. Though Shapiro's 2003 discussion of Schmitt in *Sovereign Nations, Carnal States* is more narrowly focused and less historically minded than the present volume, there he developed an understanding of Schmitt as a theorist particularly attentive to somatic politics. Like Hegel, Schmitt sees collective identity as dependent upon the harmonious combination of emotional training. For Hegel, this necessitates plural sources of affective organization (e.g., town, family, class) as well as the processes of policing that channel these sources into an organic state structure. Schmitt's challenge, on the other hand, is to build a model of sovereign authority and national unification in a period when growing social mobility and the increasing power of mass culture have undermined the stability of habits associated with Hegel's organic order.

Schmitt's fame rests on his particular theorizations of nationalism and sovereignty, which Shapiro now elaborates upon in *Carl Schmitt and the Intensification of Politics*. But it is the affective dimension of Schmitt's political theory from Shapiro's earlier book that sets the stage for the various dimensions of centralized politics he studies in the current volume. The underpinning of a successful politics, according to Schmitt, is the formal mobilization of collective emotional identifications. According to Shapiro, Schmitt takes from Sorel the idea that mythology—through its simplification of complex emotional resonances into a unified narrative—can generate energies bearing political potentialities. Where Sorel sees these narrative simplifications as mobilizing political action against capital, Schmitt sees the potential for the unification of states and people.

Schmitt therefore expands the realm of the state to clearly include art, which excites the passions and leads them into the service of the people. Far from being irrelevant, Nazi Germany's infatuation with film (for example, the expertise of Leni Riefenstahl) and aggressive posture toward the contemporary art of the period (the dissolution of the Bauhaus and the infamous "Degenerate Art" exhibition) become examples of a government looking to solidify its own aesthetic modes in the service of the German people. Shapiro describes Schmitt's argument that all of the "most varied human endeavors, from the religious, economic, moral, and other antitheses" can be utilized to develop the centralization and unification of state power. In this recognition, Shapiro argues, Schmitt allows for and encourages a vast range of contemporary theoretical investigations of bodies, micropolitics, and antipluralizations, including those of Foucault, Butler, Deleuze, Žižek, and Laclau and Mouffe.

The idea that affective intensities are a basic part of the forming of national and community identifications certainly shows their political nature. But if the political somatic holds such power, it also holds the opposite potential, the possibility to undermine the unifications of state and capital. Shapiro finds such a resource in the work of Walter Benjamin, whose recognitions of fascism's aesthetics encourage such a reversal.

The modern world has reconfigured the experience of art, Benjamin famously argued. No longer tied to spatial or temporal authenticity, the work of art has lost its claim to authority. Mechanical reproduction allows for thousands of identical paintings, the same cinematic encounter in multiple spaces and times, the domestication of the concert hall. This, in turn, dissolved the traditional "human sensory apparatus," and led to the dissolution of self-contained, authentic human being. Multiple, fragmented, confused, even perverted, forms of humanity have emerged in its place—the perverse in attempts to build or return to "authentic" cultural formulations.

Shapiro notes that Benjamin's reading of modernity could initially be mistaken for Schmitt's. However, where Schmitt hopes to subsume these various experiences into a universal state somatics, Benjamin has a more complex and more ambitious hope. On the one hand, he recognizes the increased technologization of the modern world as a constraining choice, one that even potentially eliminates the possibility of individual action. But on the other, Benjamin finds the ability to create new collectivities through these technologies. Following Marx (in function if not in form), Benjamin argues that technologies can help realize critical, even revolutionary, collectivities.

Take cinema, for example. Shapiro points to Benjamin's readings of film wherein the fragmentary social becomes a potent collectivity. Filmic representation of the commonplace—say, a domestic scene—can heighten our attention in two intriguing and related ways. The first, and most obvious, is to the particularities of existence, the commonality between putatively distant people, emphasizing their connections across time and space, which could result in a heightened sense of collective injustice and therefore action. The second, and for Shapiro more original, is to the affective and even nonsensuous aspects of potentials in life. Attention can break or reshape habits. Benjamin hopes that filmic technology can refigure the body not to create passive consumers but to activate latent revolutionary potentialities. Insofar as the response to a film (or any work of art) exceeds mere mental engagement, the excess activity transforms the audience's own visceral responses into potentiality.

"Distraction" is Benjamin's peculiar term for his hopeful somatic. The ability to be distracted, to complexly incorporate different registers of attention into one's makeup, leads to bodily potentialities. In part this is represented as an awakening from the slumber of mass capitalism, but is not an individualized, particular awakening—instead it is the concrete *reperception* of the masses toward revolutionary ends. These reperceptions, Benjamin argues, become collectively habituated, practiced, created: they configure politico-social spaces of collective existence through habituations that in and of themselves resist fascist subsumption. It is ultimately these habits that allow for a collective revolutionary consciousness to take shape.

But this cannot be a predictable consciousness; the habits of distraction cannot be predetermined. These are only potentialities, not principles. Laughter, for example, stands as an archetypal physical event, one that, for Benjamin, "provides better opportunity for thought than convulsion of the soul."[5] Laughter does not necessarily lead to a certain and formally predetermined thought; instead, it leads to the opportunity to think, the ability to notice the slippages between a statement's intention and its meaning. Laughter displaces the flawless surfaces of the modern, allowing for the emergence of critical distance and recognition of, for example, the alienation of contemporary life.

These Benjaminian understandings of somatic potential encourage Shapiro's return to Schmitt. Schmitt, like Benjamin, held an expansive vision of politics, one in which "the political" informed and depended upon a vast range of bodily experience, communal self-fashioning, and the guidance and encouragement of an *avant-garde*. For both, the people and the political are cosubstantial. Yet where Benjamin's ideals have never come to fruition (or have done so only briefly), Schmitt's have been built and rebuilt: through European fascism, nationalist movements, the building of an international system of sovereignty, political autochthonies, a half-century-long friend/ enemy distinction, wars on terror. Contemporary politics has learned Schmitt's lessons and continues to deploy them in intriguing and threatening ways. Shapiro thus returns to Schmitt for an understanding of contemporary tactics and practices, ones that combine the sensate, the affective, the ideo- logical, and the representational; in short, modern politics.

We are grateful to Niels Aaboe of Rowman & Littlefield for editorial support that has contributed significantly to enabling *Modernity and Political Thought* to successfully achieve its goals.

Kennan Ferguson, University of South Florida
Morton Schoolman, State University of New York at Albany

Notes

1. Shadia Drury, *Aquinas and Modernity: The Lost Promise of Natural Law* (Lan- ham, MD: Rowman & Littlefield, 2008); Diana Coole, *Merleau-Ponty and Modern Politics after Anti-Humanism* (Lanham, MD: Rowman & Littlefield, 2007); Kennan Ferguson, *William James: Politics in the Pluriverse* (Lanham, MD: Rowman & Little- field, 2007).

2. William E. Connolly, *The Augustinian Imperative: A Reflection on the Politics of Morality*; George Kateb, *Emerson and Self-Reliance*; Stephen K. White, *Edmund Burke: Modernity, Politics, and Aesthetics*; Tracy B. Strong, *Jean-Jacques Rousseau: The Politics of the Ordinary*; Thomas L. Dumm, *Michel Foucault and the Politics of Freedom*; Mi- chael J. Shapiro, *Reading "Adam Smith": Desire, History, and Value*; Richard E. Flath- man, *Thomas Hobbes: Skepticism, Individuality, and Chastened Politics*; Jane Bennett, *Thoreau's Nature: Ethics, Politics, and the Wild*; Fred R. Dallmayr, *G. W. F. Hegel: Modernity and Politics*; Seyla Benhabib, *The Reluctant Modernism of Hannah Arendt*. All new editions were published by Rowman & Littlefield, Inc. (Lanham) in 2002 with the exception of Benhabib's, published in 2003.

3. Kam Shapiro, *Sovereign Nations, Carnal States* (Ithaca, NY: Cornell University Press, 2003). Hereafter, page numbers will be listed parenthetically.

4. Michel Foucault, *Madness and Civilization: A History of Insanity in the Age of Reason*, trans. Richard Howard (New York: Pantheon, 1965); Pasquale Pasquino, "Theatricum Politicum: The Genealogy of Capital-Police and the State of Pros-

perity," in *The Foucault Effect: Studies in Governmentality*, ed. Graham Burchell, Colin Gordon, and Peter Miller (Brighton, UK: Harvester, 1991); Jacques Rancière, *Dis-Agreement*, trans. Julie Rose (Minneapolis: University of Minnesota Press, 1998).

5. "The Author as Producer," in *Reflections*, ed. Peter Demetz (New York: Schoken, 1986), 236.

~

Preface

In the past fifteen years, Carl Schmitt has gone from obscurity to cliché. Along with numerous translations and critical commentaries, several extensive studies of his work are now available in English.[1] It should no longer be necessary to justify a serious appraisal of his contributions to political theory (though this is still sometimes demanded). Rather than provide such a justification, or another general introduction to his writings, this book focuses on Schmitt's reformulation of sovereignty in an era of rapid technological, cultural, and social transformation. While it follows other studies by linking his work to current political questions, it also closely examines his arguments in several key works. Like most clichés, those surrounding Schmitt contain elements of truth that belie substantial underlying complications. Rather than a consistent position or a linear progression, Schmitt's political and theoretical arguments display recurrent, at times sharp vacillations. These inconsistencies are treated here as symptoms of conceptual and political *aporias* more than psychological or biographical idiosyncrasies. The study is therefore organized around Schmitt's changing responses to theoretical and political challenges to sovereign authority, roughly following a historical order. The introduction situates Schmitt's defense of sovereign authority in the context of a general philosophical and political crisis posed by the economic, cultural, and technological upheavals surrounding the crises of the interwar period. Subsequent chapters outline Schmitt's various responses to these challenges in more detail, distinguishing three main concerns: Schmitt's critique of liberalism, his formulation of an authoritarian alternative, and the turn of his gaze beyond the nation-state during and after the Second World War. Chapters 2 and 3 examine Schmitt's various attempts to recuperate sovereign authority, focusing on his shift in emphasis from Catholic jurisprudence to plebiscitary democracy and "decisionism." These attempts are often distinguished between conservative and radical, or religious and secular postures. As I argue, however, such distinctions are confounded by Schmitt's description of a supralegal executive who both represents and forms a collective will. I therefore focus on the complex techniques by which sovereign power and representation are established in both secular and religious contexts, including not only laws and institutions but also aesthetics and rhetoric. Chapter 4 takes up these concerns in Schmitt's postwar critique of international law and his analysis of partisan warfare. A final chapter ventures broader speculations regarding Schmitt's use in and relevance for contemporary discussions of global law, sovereignty, and warfare.

Notes

1. Notable studies consulted for this volume include Gopal Balakrishnan's expansive, politically oriented intellectual biography and Ellen Kennedy's historical study. George Schwab's early introduction and Joseph Bendersky's biography also remain very useful sources. Jan-Werner Müller's critical evaluation of Schmitt's European intellectual inheritance is concise, and while at times polemical, better than its title suggests. Cf. Gopal Balakrishnan, *The Enemy* (New York: Verso, 2000); Ellen Kennedy, *Constitutional Failure, Carl Schmitt in Weimar* (Durham, NC: Duke University Press, 2004); Jan-Werner Müller, A Dangerous Mind (New Haven, CT: Yale University Press, 2003); Joseph W. Bendersky, *Carl Schmitt: Theorist for the Reich* (Princeton, NJ: Princeton University Press, 1983); George Schwab, *The Challenge of the Exception* (Berlin: Duncker & Humblot, 1970).

Acknowledgments

While writing, it is easy to forget the contributions even of those on whom one most depends. I gratefully recognize some of the latter here, with a nod to all the others I omit. Morton Schoolman commissioned the book for Rowman & Littlefield and provided detailed comments at several stages. Without him it would neither have been undertaken nor completed in its current form. Many of the ideas in this study were inflected and refined through years of ongoing conversations with Jason Frank. Isabella Winkler has also been a frequent interlocutor whose recognition and critical assessments are both crucial sources of inspiration. Julie Weber provided both close readings and a broader perspective on the opening and closing chapters. For the past two years, Ana Acena has supported me in all ways, not least by reading several chapters and asking many probing questions. Jennifer Jordan and Dominik Göbel each helped me with some translation questions, though they certainly bear no responsibility for my errors. Kennan Ferguson read the work closely and offered good suggestions at later stages.

CHAPTER ONE

～

Schmitt at Large

Carl Schmitt's reemergence as a political theorist of major interest has been described as symptomatic of a return to sobriety.[1] In the decade following the events of 1989, giddy celebrations of a "new world order" composed of open markets and liberal constitutions were cut short by a proliferation of local and transnational conflicts. Starting with the ethnic cleansing and eventual partition of the former Yugoslavia—a premonition of the civil wars and genocides to follow—liberal democracies found themselves engaged in militant and polemical struggles with old enemies in new guises, and vice versa. More recently, in a global war declared against these enemies, they have mingled with religious and ethnic distinctions and compromised their own constitutions. The failure of the liberal state to contain the volatility of global markets and capture popular imaginations has inspired a familiar range of reactionary nationalism and messianic globalism. Schmitt, meanwhile, has remained topical.[2] His critical analyses of the centrifugal potentials of liberal democracy, political theology, global politics, and asymmetrical warfare, as well as his formulations of authoritarian democracy, resonate with a variety of current concerns. Yet his writings and their implications have also been the subject of sharply divergent interpretations, partly in response to a changing political climate. In the 1990s, Schmitt provided a beleaguered Left with an acute and satisfyingly contemptuous diagnosis of an ostensibly depoliticized neoliberal order. More recently, his work has been seen as foreshadowing the repoliticization of that order in an authoritarian direction.[3] For some, the move to Schmitt is symptomatic of threats posed to secular pluralism and

1

the neutral state by demands for stronger forms of popular sovereignty and political identity (on both Left and Right).[4] For a few, Schmitt inadvertently provides resources for a radical democratic pluralism.[5]

Schmitt has thus become a diffractive surface for contemporary political debates, more frequently serving as an "affectively charged symbol" than an object of critical analysis.[6] While his work has become widely available, it is more often cited than closely read. In this respect it is hardly unique, as textual interpretations are always in some respects polemical acts on the part of motivated parties. Nor would Schmitt himself likely have been surprised by the diversity of his appropriations. Indeed, as I will argue further, one could very well apply Schmitt's analysis of polemical interpretations to current deployments of his own writings. However, his work is particularly susceptible to controversy, due to its peculiar combination of a highly charged historical situation, interdisciplinarity, and political ambivalence. Schmitt criticized liberal democracy from a variety of perspectives amidst its greatest crisis and failure, playing a complex role in the evolution and eventual collapse of the Weimar Republic before joining the Nazi Party in 1933. While consistently antiliberal, Schmitt demonstrated persistent uncertainties regarding the limits and possibilities of constitutional, religious, and popular sources of sovereign authority and power.

As Gopal Balakrishnan has suggested, part of Schmitt's appeal is that the elusiveness of his position reflects that of our own.[7] Many of the challenges Schmitt faced, while especially acute, remain familiar. His career illustrates the possibilities and dangers involved in a reconstruction of democratic sovereignty in an age of military, economic, and social dislocation. In addition to their political relevance, his writings combine historical and sociological analysis, metaphysical interpretation, and polemical rhetoric. They therefore comprise a fascinating intersection of discursive and political strategies. In the rest of this chapter, I examine this intersection, focusing on Schmitt's efforts to distinguish a source of popular sovereignty in an age of global flows and social complexity. As I argue, a close analysis of these efforts reveals a complex set of tactics and dissimulations at work not only in Schmitt's texts, but also in the practice of sovereign power and representation.

Schmitt composed his best-known works amidst the violent political and economic upheavals following the first wave of capitalist globalization and its collapse with the First World War. In these works, Schmitt described a general crisis of state sovereignty resulting from the combined challenges of corporate capital, international political organizations, bureaucratic administration, organized social groups, and the emergence of mass culture in the wake of new technologies of communication. Above all, Schmitt sought to prevent the sovereign state from being absorbed by these groups and forces. The state, for Schmitt, was properly a site of "*pouvoir constituant*" (constituent power), responsible for collective will-formation and its constitutional expression, though his understanding of the exact relationship between law and power varied over time. In his defense of the sovereign state, Schmitt struggled with the threats to political autonomy highlighted by Hegel, and especially Max Weber, with whom he had studied. On one hand, centralized legislation and decision-making were jeopardized by the plurality of bureaucratic functions and agencies required to manage bourgeois economies and the social order in which they were pervasively integrated (what Schmitt came to call the "quantitative total state").[8] On the other hand, liberal society was itself being organized into various "social" groups, particularly capital and labor associations that, in turn, were channeled by political parties. Just as flexible and rapid administrative reactions were necessitated by foreign and domestic pressures, along with rapid military, economic, and technological developments, the autonomy of the political administration (not to mention journalists and academics) was jeopardized by competing parties and unstable coalitions. Rather than integrating antagonized social groups, public policy and law were instrumentalized by them, or by professional politicians seeking their votes. As Schmitt described it, the depoliticization of government was met with the politicization of society.[9]

Along with these general challenges, the parliamentary system of the Weimar Republic suffered a unique combination of domestic and international pressures. Not only was the Republic itself a new government, parliament had always been a weak source of national integration in Germany due to its history of estate-based representation. The Weimar Constitution did not distinguish political parties from economic associations, preventing them from serving as "organs of popular will-formation."[10] Moreover, popular faith in liberal tenets of representation and rational will-formation had been shattered by the collapse of the European state system, the devastating violence of World War I and the economic crises of its aftermath. Other factors included cultural conflicts aroused by the avant-garde culture of Weimar Berlin and the Republic's association with a humiliating capitulation to foreign powers after military defeat.[11] Liberal elites were ill prepared to manage the combination of these crises with the dynamics of mass politics. As Max Horkheimer described it, the republican government was characterized by fragmented bureaucratic offices and lacked charismatic leadership.[12] Under these conditions, radical parties (Bolshevik or Fascist) were able not only to capture political offices, but even to mount direct challenges to the state outside legal channels.[13] Finally, in the aftermath of Versailles, corporate capital and foreign powers imposed severe military and economic sanctions on the administration, forcing budgetary adjustments and jeopardizing its claims to autonomy.

Schmitt's various responses to these challenges derive an impression of coherence from their common opposition to liberalism. From the perspective of classical liberalism, Schmitt noted, sovereign authority is a contradiction, as a lawful order is presumed to result from the free association of private individuals or the deliberation of parliamentary representatives, governed only by neutral rules and procedures. Schmitt's rejection of the neutral state and his commitment to personal authority were thoroughgoing and strongly motivated, taking metaphysical, historical, and palpably aesthetic forms. He rejected out of hand any immanent or organic synthesis of interests and values, whether in parliament or the public sphere, both of which he associated with outmoded Enlightenment models of rational consensus. He found the prospect of democratic integration from below, much less a democratic pluralism, inconceivable. One might say he was pathologically skeptical of democratic or republican virtue. However, he shared this attitude not only with a distinguished reactionary tradition but also with contemporary critics from across the political spectrum. The rationalist pretense that parliamentary procedures generate public consensus by resolving social conflicts through shared norms of discussion and debate, Schmitt noted, had been widely discredited in an age of party propaganda, mass media, bureaucratic specialization, professional politicians, and violent class struggle. Authors as diverse as Lenin, Sorel, and Walter Lippman described an irrational public that was an alternately passive and volatile conduit of emotion and power. Rather than a source of democratic identity, parliament had become an echo chamber for the chaotic struggles of social and economic factions. Nor was any of this lost on a public disenchanted, insecure, and (especially in the case of military veterans) traumatized by the horrors of the First World War. Rather than a sphere of discussion and rational consensus, as Schmitt observed, parliament was (justly enough) viewed with cynicism or suspicion, seen as a more or less transparent screen for factional competition and elite control.

Dismissing the liberal conceit of a "self-organizing" society, Schmitt sought a political authority capable of integrating fractured groups and interests. The source and nature of this authority varied. However, Schmitt consistently refused to sublimate sovereign power in mechanical conventions or procedures. As Ellen Kennedy has argued, Schmitt therefore repudiated both formalism and realism. Each reduce politics to "facts," whether a legal constitution or a socio-economic (and territorial) *status quo*, and so hypostasize either the will or the body of the people, rendering themselves unfit in times of radical transformation.[14] During Weimar, Schmitt was especially critical of legal positivism, exemplified by the jurist Hans Kelsen. Legal norms, Schmitt emphasized, rested on a corresponding social order—a "normal situation"—and so ultimately depended upon judicial or political decisions regarding when to adopt them in the first place, to determine the proper circumstances of their application, or ultimately to suspend them in the face of a more general threat to order as such.[15] He thus sought a source of such decisions beyond the reach of the unruly forces of the market, parliamentary parties, and social movements. Practically speaking, this came to mean a relatively independent personal executive who could identify and respond to constitutional challenges by radical parties, economic interests, or international enemies with a broad range of economic, military, and police powers.

As a public legal theorist, Schmitt focused especially on the constitutional definition of executive power in the "state of exception" (*Ausnahmezustand*). In the critical situation he occupied, extensive powers were required (and not infrequently used as provided under Article 48 of the Weimar constitution) to ward off threats to the social and institutional *status quo*.[16] Initially, such measures were invoked to deal with violent civil conflict and later to manage economic adjustments necessitated by international debts and the global depression. Indeed, in Weimar "Crises . . . were the rule rather than the exception."[17] Yet even in these circumstances, Schmitt's preoccupation with the possession and exercise of supralegal authority stands out. As he famously wrote in *Political Theology*, "The exception is more interesting than the rule. The rule proves nothing; the exception proves everything: It confirms not only the rule but also its existence, which derives from the exception. In the exception the power of real life breaks through the crust of a mechanism that has become torpid by repetition."[18] Schmitt is thus commonly associated with the subordination of legal norms to sovereign, personal power.[19] However, as Balakrishnan has argued, Schmitt was also deeply concerned with the "nebulous factor of 'legitimacy'" linking power, law, and a substantial order, though their relationship often remained obscure in his own writings.[20] Sovereign power was constitutive in that it identified and shaped the conditions in which norms applied. It was legitimate, or "representative," in that it thereby served, or as Schmitt would have it, *conserved* the unity of law and a higher order, however conceived. Even when promoting executive supremacy, Schmitt adopted a conservative rather than revolutionary posture, one he associated with the figure of the *Katechon*, or "restrainer" of the apocalypse described in Paul's second letter to the Thessalonians. Schmitt's challenge was to elevate sovereign power above abstract norms or volatile interests, and at the same time to maintain its status (or its appearance) as representative of an underlying (or overarching) unity, or, in the form of the oft-cited paradox, to put exceptional authority in the service of a normal situation.

How could sovereign power over dynamic technological and economic processes be extracted from struggles between antagonized social interests and at the same time be (democratically) legitimated? In the brief, volatile history of the Republic, Schmitt's attempts to resolve tensions between political form and constituent power, or norm and exception, shifted between Catholic rationalism and authoritarian nationalism, constitutional reform and conservative revolution. Balakrishnan suggests Schmitt's shifts in position and perspective reflected the instability of his times—the absence of a "hegemonic center of gravity"—as well as his changing institutional affiliations. These factors, for example, make sense of Schmitt's reversion to a more robust constitutionalism in his *Verfassungslehre*, which he composed during the relative stability of the Republic between 1924 and the economic collapse of 1929.[21] They make less sense of his relativistic approach to sovereignty in *The Concept of the Political*, the first version of which was composed at roughly the same time. In the following chapter, I trace key aspects of these shifts in several texts from the early twenties to early thirties. However, rather than emphasizing biographical or tactical explanations for Schmitt's changing perspectives,[22] I focus on the details of his arguments, which reveal a dynamic conception of the relationship between tradition and innovation, norm and decision, organic traditions and their strategic deployment. In particular, I explicate this dynamic conception through a comparison of three instances in which it appears: The Catholic *Complexio Oppositorum* (1923); the Marxist myth of class struggle and its nationalist variant (1923); and the "polemical" opposition of friend and enemy (1932).

Placing these instances along a continuum, I argue Schmitt's work in the late 1920s and early 1930s combines a search for legitimate sovereignty with an increasing sense of its synthetic character. Along these lines, I read Schmitt's development around his claim in *Political Theology* that "all law is situational."[23] That is, I interpret his move toward "relative" models of sovereign power as an adjustment to the heightened pace of social disintegration, a move that culminated in his turn to decisionism and plebiscitary dictatorship. As this approach makes clear, George Schwab's characterization of this movement as a transition from "the church, the possessor of *veritas*, to the state, the possessor of *potestas*" obscures tensions in both Schmitt's religious and secular models of sovereign authority.[24] In both cases, the paradox of the sovereign exception, whereby political power shapes the underlying ideas, interests, and values it purports to express, at once "representing" and "constituting" political form, was negotiated rather than dissolved by a clear choice between the two. In short, I argue legitimate or "representative" authority was not abandoned, nor simply reasserted, but instead transformed, its source shifting from an ethos of belief to a pathos of identification.

Rather than accuse Schmitt of self-contradiction, then, my aim is to elucidate the techniques by which he reformulates his defense of sovereign authority. In the mid-1920s Schmitt largely abandoned his search for traditional (Catholic) authority in favor of a leader who could both draw from and direct the energies of mass democracy. However, he drew a parallel between divine and democratic modes of constituent power. Neither the Will of God nor that of the People are reducible to positive statutes, nor can either speak directly; each require a representative authorized to make extralegal political decisions. Hence, both Catholic and democratic sovereignty rest on popular faith in a visible figure who represents an invisible order. But whence such faith in a secular, pluralistic society? As parliament had lost any plausible connection to a unified public, Schmitt turned to the executive. In collective hostility to a common enemy, and in the popular trust (*Vertrauen*) of the people in the personal competence of their leader, Schmitt found sources of "form" that rendered constituent power representative yet largely unaccountable, thus facilitating broad discretion in response to social conflicts. In Schmitt's turn to what is sometimes seen as a "relativistic" model of political authority, we thus find a continuum along which the substance of legitimacy becomes increasingly vague, dissolved of content to the point where ultimately—starting with *The Concept of the Political*—a sovereign decision mobilizes an amorphous fund of popular energies, a kind of standing reserve of affective intensity.

Whether Schmitt imagined that popular acclaim placed supralegal authority in the service of substantial forms of collective life (whether ideological, cultural, or racial) or was itself shaped by political action and rhetoric was not always clear. As I argue, this uncertainty is inherent to the dynamic relationship between form and power outlined above. However, in his attempts to establish legitimate authority, Schmitt dissimulated such complexities and contradictions. Indeed, this dissimulation was central to his depiction of the personal authority of the executive as more properly "representative" than parliament, perhaps the most properly fascist aspect of his writing prior to 1933 (after which he took up the legal defense of Hitler's rule and a more vulgar anti-Semitism).[25] Hence, his earlier formulations of constituent power are understandably read in the light of his subsequent justification of Hitler's executive supremacy. While it has been convincingly argued that this was not Schmitt's ultimate aim (at the time, emergency measures were used precisely to prevent a capture of legal power by anticonstitutional parties),[26] critics such as William Scheuerman and John McCormick are justified in describing Schmitt's jurisprudence as *logically* consistent with fascism. In any case, it harmonized with fascist modes of juridical self-representation. In *Legality and Legitimacy* (1932) Schmitt described presidential plebiscites as a form of "substantial" legislation, thus dissolving distinctions between law and decree, altering and destroying the constitution, as well as legal and personal authority.[27]

Schmitt's readers have attributed differing levels of self-consciousness to his complicity with Nazism, depicting him as opportunistic, earnest, or naive by turns.[28] Simona Draghici, for example, finds Schmitt "persistently puzzled" by the "indefinite extension" of the exception.[29] William Scheuerman argues "Schmitt's marriage to Nazism stems immanently from core elements of his jurisprudence."[30] Yet these are not mutually contradictory possibilities. As Schmitt understood, jurisprudential norms cannot strictly determine the course of their practical applications, each of which can be figured, *ex post facto*, as an expression of legal principles. Nazism necessarily arose upon a plurality of enabling conditions without therefore being preordained.[31] Giorgio Agamben mistakes logic for destiny when—opposing Schmitt's attempt to render the exception to a juridical category—he argues "the end of the Weimar Republic clearly demonstrates that . . . a 'protected democracy' is not a democracy at all, and that the paradigm of constitutional dictatorship functions instead as a transitional phase that leads inevitably to the establishment of a totalitarian regime."[32]

Regardless of how one interprets Schmitt's accommodation to Nazism after 1933, however, his prior depiction of an independent source of decision belied a political reality of which he could hardly have been unaware. In the early thirties, prior to Hitler's appointment as chancellor, Article 48 was invoked to support the essentially bureaucratic rule, or "economic dictatorship" of Brüning and Hindenberg.[33] As Chris Thornhill argues, Schmitt's defense of sovereign dignity was therefore linked to the same technical resolutions of antagonism he denigrated in parliamentary rule. "Despite Schmitt's (self-proclaimed) hostility to merely technical or administrative politics . . . his critique of technical government has little more than a metaphorical or gestural quality."[34] Yet these gestures nonetheless served a vital purpose. While dispensing with the substantial order he describes in his Catholic writings, Schmitt's turn to formalistic decisionism with its superficial, yet absolute legitimation "provides the perfect model for the fluid, non-substantive codes of an authoritarian bureaucracy."[35] As Catherine Colliot-Thelene argues, the instrumentalization of law is not thereby restrained so much as "*hidden* by the suppleness of belief."[36] Needless to say, the capture of public belief was a crucial value for Schmitt. Like Weber, he may have hoped to link a charismatic executive to a technocratic administration, thus containing the energies of mass politics in relatively stable institutional and legal forms. Many of the conservative elites who supported Hitler had similar misapprehensions. As John McCormick has argued, Schmitt's history reveals the extreme dangers of this approach. Rather than channeling collective antagonisms in stable institutions, fascism amplified and destabilized them, mobilizing a rapid substitution of symbols and enemies, each of which became so many occasions for the synthesis of political form and will. In the course of a chaotic, excessive drive for legitimacy, administrative apparatuses and technologies became instruments of imperialist war and genocidal violence.

Despite Schmitt's overarching commitment to sovereign authority, then, it is not easy to summarize his approach. His work is characterized not only by fluctuating political postures but also a complex blend of form and genre, including medieval theology, constitutional law, sociology, history, and psychology. In particular, the persistence of theological terms in Schmitt's later writings is a major source of their ambiguity, further complicating the shift from traditional elites to plebiscitary mass democracy. As a result, a definitive account of Schmitt's theory of the exception or "the political" has proved elusive, and his commitments have been variously described as religious, aesthetic, or strategic.[37] These controversies indicate a complex relationship between these terms and their mutual refashioning in Schmitt's arguments. More generally, I argue, the inextricability of these terms in Schmitt's writings mirrors their practical combination in political action. Some of Schmitt's closer readers have therefore dispensed with attempts to privilege one perspective or another and instead explored their interplay in his texts. For different reasons, Jan-Werner Müller thus dismisses any search for an "essence" to Schmitt's thinking,[38] and Balakrishnan describes Schmitt as an intellectual "bricoleur," and political "schizophrenic," characterizing his *oeuvre*—borrowing Schmitt's own terms—as an "explosively unstable combination . . . *Complexio Oppositorum*."[39] In his testimony at Nuremburg, Schmitt described what he called the "Carl Schmitt myth" in similar fashion: "Carl Schmitt is quite a peculiar individual, not just a professor; he is also a composite of various other individuals."[40]

Schmitt's challenge was to generate coherence out of the same combination of ideas and perspectives that renders his own work so "explosive." Both his successes and failures are instructive. As Müller points out, Schmitt effectively combined pragmatic simplicity with a capacious use of metaphor and hyperbole. Comparing Schmitt to Burke, he argues, "Language was to persuade and even to mobilize—its aesthetic quality was essential, not accidental."[41] It could thus be argued that the aesthetic, rhetorical, and gestural dimensions of Schmitt's theory of sovereignty are those most urgently in need of analysis. Rather than accuse Schmitt of aestheticizing politics, I suggest one can find in his work a very useful illustration of aesthetic dimensions of present forms of popular sovereignty, that is, the various ways a democratic people are symbolically and rhetorically constituted and linked to political authority. Schmitt's vacillations between harsh objectivity and surplus passion (Balakrishnan) or "realism and impressionism" (Müller) mimic the fraught combination in modern politics of administrative power and popular enthusiasm.[42] His attempt to distinguish legitimacy from propaganda, law from power, and conservative from revolutionary politics can be seen as an ironic, or tragic, demonstration of their entanglement. Yet Schmitt also illustrates the means by which such entanglement serves political power, particularly in his discussions of myth, oratory, and the historical role of religious imagery.[43] Finally, his combination of strategic, polemical, and critical perspectives provides us with an instructive guide to their interplay in political struggles.

It could be said that Schmitt never achieved the resignation to the contradictory imperatives of Utopia and realism in modern politics that E. H. Carr found missing in Weimar politics more generally.[44] However, it remains unclear today just what form such a resignation might take. Relationships between power, law, and democratic identity remain highly uncertain. Schmitt's arguments for executive autonomy have been read as apt precedents not only for fascism but also contemporary modes of government faced with destabilizing global flows of commerce, labor, and media. As Ingeborg Maus has argued, "[The] idea of a dynamic and deformalized law for which Schmitt gave a theoretical foundation is today what we have in practice in all spheres of the law."[45] William Scheuerman similarly finds a variety of correlates of Schmitt's notion of "motorized legislation" in contemporary executive and administrative rule.[46] As was the case in Weimar, current concentrations of power in the executive branch and the expansion of a discretionary administration not only undermine popular accountability, but have also failed to produce a stable social and economic order. Michael Hardt, Antonio Negri, and Giorgio Agamben have gone further, arguing that the rule of law over a stable territorial order may no longer describe the "normal" exercise of sovereignty. Instead, they claim contemporary forms of global sovereignty operate in a "permanent state of exception."[47]

These last concerns are the subject of the final chapters of this book, which deal with Schmitt's exploration of alternatives to the nation-state in the aftermath of Germany's defeat in the Second World War and consider contemporary parallels. In *The Nomos of the Earth* (1950), Schmitt once again found legal norms detached from a normal situation.[48] The correspondence between international law and a "concrete order" of European political institutions and customs was jeopardized by the effects of expanded transnational economic and political forces on domestic cultural and economic relations. These effects were exacerbated by the contradictory policies of the United States under the Monroe Doctrine, which fixed legal boundaries while undermining the sociological substance on which they rested. As we have already seen, Schmitt's emphasis on constituent power was at odds not only with legal formalism but also sociological positivism. By way of an etymology of *nomos*, Schmitt established a complex model of territoriality that reiterates the dynamic relationship between power and form outlined above at a transnational scale. International law also rests on substantial relations between collectives that are shaped, in turn, by economic, military, and cultural technologies and practices. In the face of intensified global economies and political forms, Schmitt thus moved beyond the nation-state. However, he retained his critique of positive norms asserted in the absence of a genuine correspondence of "order and location" (*Ordnung und Ortung*). In particular, Schmitt rejected a global order in favor of a new plurality of interstate federations or "*Grossräum,*" a notion previously adapted to justify Hitler's expansionist policies. Schmitt's critique of international law highlights the danger of a pretense to legality on the part of great powers, a critique some might find ironic given his earlier complicity with such pretensions. Potential conflict between unstable groupings can only be limited, but never ruled out, he argues, if international norms are subtended by substantial economic, military, and cultural relations that mitigate antagonism. Within a space so constituted, one finds limited forms of war undertaken by "just enemies." As I argue, Schmitt's formulations of just enemies and "bracketed" antagonism function as an implicit critique of his earlier focus on a univocal sovereign. In the process, they clarify the relationship between universal norms and political pluralism, revealing complex processes and techniques out of which friends and enemies emerge and by which the violence of their differences can be amplified or mitigated. In Schmitt's late work, *The Theory of the Partisan* (1963), these insights are brought to bear on the phenomena of partisan, or irregular, warfare. As Schmitt argues, a dynamic combination of legal, rhetorical, and strategic factors drive the channeling of local, bracketed grievances into global ideological polarities. In a concluding chapter, I consider the implications of this discussion for debates surrounding the definition of enemies in the "war on terror."

Notes

1. See Paul Piccone and G. L. Ulmen, "Introduction to Carl Schmitt," *Telos* 72 (Summer 1987): 12. They write, "Schmitt's cold realism can be a healthy corrective to the Heideggerian inebriation," one they see taken up in "the narcotics of post-modernism." Cf. Gopal Balakrishnan, *The Enemy* (New York: Verso, 2000), 268. On the "timely" response Schmitt offers to an "inebriating" consensus, see 261.

2. Frederic Jameson, for example, refers to the "astonishing contemporaneity" of Schmitt's *The Nomos of the Earth*. Cf. Jameson, "Notes on Nomos," *South Atlantic Quarterly* 104.2 (Spring 2005): 199. See also Simona Draghici, "Preface," in Carl Schmitt, *Four Articles*, trans. Simona Draghici (Corvallis, OR: Plutarch Press, 1999), vii; Ellen Kennedy, *Constitutional Failure, Carl Schmitt in Weimar* (Durham, NC: Duke University Press, 2004), 3; G. L. Ulmen, "Introduction to Schmitt," *Roman Catholicism and Political Form*, trans. G. L. Ulmen (Westport, CT: Greenwood Press, 1996), ix.

3. Cf. Michael Hardt and Antonio Negri, *Empire* (Cambridge, MA: Harvard University Press, 2000); Giorgio Agamben, *State of Exception*, trans. Kevin Attell (Chicago: University of Chicago Press, 2005). Consider also the following title: Renato Cristi, *Carl Schmitt and Authoritarian Liberalism: Strong State, Free Economy* (Cardiff: University of Wales Press, 1998).

4. Cf. Richard Wolin, "Carl Schmitt: The Conservative Revolutionary Habitus and the Aesthetics of Horror," *Political Theory* 20 (1992): 424–47; Jan-Werner Müller, *A Dangerous Mind* (New Haven, CT: Yale University Press, 2003); Heinrich Meier, *The Lesson of Carl Schmitt* (Chicago: University of Chicago Press, 1998).

5. Chantal Mouffe, in particular, conscripts Schmitt for a polemical reconstruction of democratic pluralism (her argument will be discussed in chapter 5). Cf. Chantal Mouffe, *The Return of the Political* (New York: Verso, 1993); Mouffe, *The Democratic Paradox* (New York: Verso, 2000).

6. See Balakrishnan, *The Enemy*, 9.

7. Balakrishnan, *The Enemy*, 136.

8. Cf. Schmitt, "Further Development of the Total State in Germany," *Four Articles*, 22; George Schwab, *The Challenge of the Exception* (Berlin: Duncker & Humblot, 1970), 140.

9. Cf. Schmitt, "The Way to the Total State," in Schmitt, *Four Articles*, 9: "The parties in which various societal interests and trends organize themselves are the very society turned into a multi-party state."

10. Cf. Chris Thornhill, *Political Theory in Modern Germany* (Cambridge, UK: Polity Press, 1999), 41.

11. Cf. George Paxton, *The Anatomy of Fascism* (New York: Vintage Books, 2005), 77–78.

12. Cf. Max Horkheimer, "Changes in the Structure of Political Compromise," *The Essential Frankfurt School Reader* (New York: Continuum, 1982), 65.

13. Cf. Balakrishnan, *The Enemy*, 151.

14. Kennedy, *Constitutional Failure*, 6.

15. Cf. Schmitt, *Political Theology*, trans. George Schwab (Cambridge, MA: MIT Press, 1988), 13, hereafter cited as *PT*.

16. For a discussion of Article 48, see Schwab, *Challenge*, 37.

17. Schwab, *Challenge*, 29.

18. Carl Schmitt, *PT*, 15.

19. Thus, Ellen Kennedy refers to "the central element of sovereignty for Carl Schmitt: The personal action of the commander." Cf. Kennedy, *Constitutional Failure*, 81–82.

20. Balakrishnan, *The Enemy*, 46. Guy Oakes similarly claims, "Schmitt's view of the exact relationship between decisions and norms was never entirely clear." Oakes, "Introduction to Schmitt," *Political Romanticism*, trans. Guy Oakes (Cambridge, MA: MIT Press, 1986), xxxv, fn. 20. Kennedy writes, "he is torn between decisionist and normative theory." Cf. Kennedy, *Constitutional Failure*, 71.

21. Carl Schmitt, *Verfassungslehre* (Munchen: Duncker & Humblot, 1928).

22. For an example of this approach, see Ingeborg Maus, "The 1933 'Break' in Carl Schmitt's Theory," in *Law as Politics*, ed. Dyzenhaus (Durham, NC: Duke University Press, 1998): 196–216.

23. Schmitt, *PT*, 13.

24. Schwab, *Challenge*, 135.

25. Among other things, Schmitt notoriously defended Hitler's 1934 purge, which involved the murder of some of Schmitt's former friends and associates, in "The Führer Protects the Law." Cf. Joseph Bendersky, *Carl Schmitt, Theorist for the Reich* (Princeton, NJ: Princeton University Press, 1983), part IV; Kennedy, *Constitutional Failure*, 23; Schwab, *Challenge*, 118.

26. See Schwab, *Challenge*, 43. See also Joseph Bendersky, "Carl Schmitt and the Conservative Revolution," *Telos* 72 (Summer 1987): 27–42; Bendersky, *Carl Schmitt*, 119.

27. Carl Schmitt, *Legality and Legitimacy*, trans and ed. Jeffrey Seitzer (Durham, NC: Duke University Press, 2004).

28. Both Guy Oakes and Jan-Werner Müller highlight Schmitt's retrospective dissimulations—whether deceptive or self-deceptive—of his work. See Oakes, "Preface," Carl Schmitt, *Political Romanticism*, trans. Guy Oakes (Cambridge, MA: MIT Press, 1986). On Schmitt's propagation of the "Benito Cereno" myth, see Müller, *A Dangerous Mind*, 57. On Schmitt's turn to Nazism, see Schwab, *Challenge*, 106–7 and Müller, *A Dangerous Mind*, 37. On his anti-Semitism, see Kennedy, *Constitutional Failure*, 226–29; Bendersky, *Carl Schmitt*, 208, 227–42; Schwab, *Challenge*, 133–38.

Piccone and Ulmen, like Bendersky, see Schmitt's anti-Semitism as opportunistic, and theoretically epiphenomenal. See Piccone and Ulmen, "Introduction to Carl Schmitt," 11. Ellen Kennedy sees Schmitt as trying to protect himself from academic competitors and enemies. Cf. Kennedy, *Constitutional Failure*, 24. For a different view, see Raphael Gross, *Carl Schmitt and the Jews*, trans. Joel Golb (Madison: University of Wisconsin Press, 2007).

29. Schmitt, *Four Articles*, xiii. See also Thornhill, *Political Theory*, 85 on Schmitt's "spectacular" misapprehension of Nazi politics.

30. William Scheuerman, *Carl Schmitt* (Lanham, MD: Rowman & Littlefield, 1999), 114.

31. Cf. George Paxton, *The Anatomy of Fascism* (New York: Vintage Books, 2005), 39, 53–54; Jacob Taubes, *The Political Theology of Paul*, trans. Dana Hollander (Stanford, CA: Stanford University Press, 2004), 102; Kennedy, *Constitutional Failure*, 8. Along these lines, it may be pointed out that religious anti-Semitism (such as Schmitt's) need not imply racial anti-Semitism, though it can nonetheless join it in a common cause.

32. Giorgio Agamben, *State of Exception*, trans. Kevin Attell (Chicago: University of Chicago Press, 2005), 15.

33. Cf. Thornhill, *Political Theory*, 76; Balakrishnan, *The Enemy*, 148. Ingeborg Maus, "The 1933 'Break' in Carl Schmitt's Theory," 197. On Schmitt's popularity with industrial elite at the time, see Jan-Werner Müller, *A Dangerous Mind*, 37.

34. Thornhill, *Political Theory*, 76.

35. Thornhill, *Political Theory*, 80.

36. Catherine Colliot-Thélene, "Carl Schmitt versus Max Weber," in *The Challenge of Carl Schmitt*, ed. Chantal Mouffe (New York: Verso, 1999), 140. As Balakrishnan notes, "the Finance Ministry, which Schmitt held up as a bastion of independent statehood . . . had been doling out massive subsidies to heavy industry." Balakrishnan, *The Enemy*, 150.

37. Richard Wolin describes Schmitt's commitment to the exception as "aesthetic," comparing it to Nietzsche's conception of aesthetic self-creation. Cf. Wolin, "Carl Schmitt, The Conservative Revolutionary Habitus and the Aesthetics of Horror," *Political Theory* 20.3 (August 1992): 434. For Leo Strauss, on the other hand, "the affirmation of the political is in the last analysis nothing other than the affirmation of the moral." Cf. Strauss, "Comments on Carl Schmitt's *Der Begriff des Politischen*," in Schmitt, Concept of the Political, 99.

38. Jan-Werner Müller, *A Dangerous Mind*, 6.

39. Balakrishnan, *The Enemy*, 136 and 259, respectively. See also Kennedy, *Constitutional Failure*, 5–6.

40. Quoted in Joseph Bendersky, "Schmitt at Nuremberg," *Telos* 72 (Summer 1987): 91–129, 103.

41. Jan-Werner Müller, *A Dangerous Mind*, 9.

42. Balakrishnan, *Enemy*, 261; Jan-Werner Müller, *A Dangerous Mind*, 9. Stephen Holmes similarly refers to Schmitt's "mixture of sober insight and apocalyptic pretension" (Schmitt, *Political Romanticism*, back cover).

43. See Schmitt, *Roman Catholicism and Political Form*. Along these lines, Piccone and Ulmen suggest Schmitt's socio-political contextualization of art "might well provide a challenging point of departure for a cultural critique in the West and a critical culture in the East." Cf. "Introduction to Carl Schmitt," 13.

44. E. H. Carr, *The Twenty Years' Crisis* (New York: Harper and Row, 1964), 93.

45. Ingeborg Maus, "The 1933 'Break' in Carl Schmitt's Theory," 197.

46. See William Scheuerman, *Liberal Democracy and the Social Acceleration of Time* (Baltimore, MD: Johns Hopkins University Press, 2004).

47. Cf. Michael Hardt and Antonio Negri, *Empire* (Cambridge, MA: Harvard University Press, 2000), 18; Giorgio Agamben, *State of Exception*, trans. Kevin Attell (Chicago: University of Chicago Press, 2005), 14.

48. Carl Schmitt, *The Nomos of the Earth*, trans. G. L. Ulmen (New York: Telos, 2003); Carl Schmitt, *Der Nomos der Erde im Volkerrecht des Jus Publicum Europaeum* (Berlin: Dunker & Humblot, 1997).

CHAPTER TWO

~

Channels of Political Authority

In the political climate of the early 1920s, Schmitt's critique of parliamentary deliberation as a rational means of democratic will-formation had the powerful resonance of common sense. Mass democracy, corporate capital, and a world war had combined to render the liberal image of a "self-organizing society" (whether in the form of parliamentary discussion or a free market) hollow, if not pathetic. In Weimar, antagonized social and economic groupings had colonized the parliamentary state, which became a battlefield for disciplined, hierarchical parties. In his introduction to the first edition of *The Crisis of Parliamentary Democracy* in 1923, Schmitt describes the resulting perception of parliament in terms that still sound perfectly contemporary. "Finally, even nonsocialists recognize the collusion of press, party, and capital and treated politics only as a shadow of economic reality."[1] Parliament, he concludes, had "lost its moral and intellectual foundation and only remains standing through sheer mechanical perseverance as an empty apparatus."[2] With the loss of confidence in rational discussion, parliament was no longer seen to synthesize a democratic General Will from antagonized social groupings. Insofar as it had rested on this confidence, moreover, the link between liberalism and democracy had always been tenuous. As Schmitt argues, belief in rational discussion had never itself been strictly rational. In terms that would later become central to his *Concept of the Political*, he claims that rather than stemming from common or overlapping values, the identification of liberalism and democracy had been sustained by a *polemical* bond against a common enemy. "So long as it was essentially a polemical concept (that

17

is, the negation of established monarchy), democratic convictions could be joined to and reconciled with various other political aspirations. But to the extent that it was realized, democracy was seen to serve many masters and not in any way to have a substantial, clear goal."[3]

The Republic had become a form without content. Or rather, it was a fragile vessel rent by proliferating struggles. Mechanical perseverance would not keep it standing for long. Among the parties competing for power were the Bolsheviks (KPD) and the Nazis (NSDAP), both of whom garnered popular support by focusing popular resentments against parliament. Schmitt himself ultimately supported the suspension of parliament in favor of emergency rule by a virtually autonomous executive. However, he consistently framed his support for discretionary powers in conservative terms, describing the executive as a "defender" of the constitutional order.[4] In the terms he established in *Die Diktatur* (1921)—where he considered the presidential emergency powers authorized under Article 48 in light of the history of constitutional provisions authorizing temporary dictatorships—Schmitt advocated "commissarial" rather than "sovereign" dictatorship.[5] The commissarial dictator, traced to Roman legal traditions, protects the constitutional in its "concrete duration," [*konkreten Bestand*] suspending law in order to reestablish the practical conditions on which it depends.[6] The sovereign dictator, by contrast, appeared in the French Revolution, where his authority was grounded in the "*pouvoir constituant*" of the people, making him the source of law itself.[7]

Schmitt's attempt to distinguish commissarial from sovereign dictatorship had an immediate contemporary application, namely the defense of the Republic against radical challengers, particularly the Bolsheviks. As Schmitt argued, the Republic required an executive authorized to suspend constitutional procedures—particularly the "equal chance" of anti-Republican parties to gain power through elections—in the event of a threat to the constitutional order as a whole. The role of the executive in a state of emergency, as he had it, was to establish the boundaries within which law garnered legitimacy and obedience. However, the means and scope of exceptional powers required remained uncertain and were, in principle, impossible to formalize. Just what was required to create social stability or popular loyalty to the Republic in the divisive and volatile conditions of Weimar, and how was the executive equipped to decide?

Exception and Paradox

While his repudiation of an unbounded sovereign dictatorship—as in the Bolshevik "dictatorship of the proletariat"—is clear enough, Schmitt's attempts to incorporate the exception in a conservative framework can appear confusing, or even incoherent.[8] At times they appear to rest on an unrealistic or dangerous Rousseauean model of community. "Democracy requires . . . first homogeneity and second—if the need arises—elimination or eradication of heterogeneity."[9] Yet Schmitt—like Rousseau—understood that democratic identity was always at some level a fiction, inasmuch as the people are sociologically heterogeneous. The identity of a people, Schmitt emphasizes, is not denotative but constitutive. "It is not a matter of something actually equal legally, politically or sociologically, but rather of identifications."[10] In terms Schmitt borrows from Abbé Sieyes, the identification of the people issues not from the natural unity of a race or class, but from their own constituent power (*"pouvoir constituant"*), a power that precedes and forms a constituted order.[11] Only, this would reverse the order of homogeneity and exclusion, making the elimination of heterogeneity prior to democratic homogeneity. Democratic will-formation would thus become an act prior to its author, or as Schmitt puts it, "only political power, which should come from the people's will, can form the people's will in the first place."[12]

The paradoxical character of Schmitt's notion of the exception—a suspension of constitutional norms in the name of their preservation—has often been noted. While they resist logical solutions, however, paradoxes rarely prove fatal to authority, obedience, or collective identification, none of which need be logical. As Schmitt points out, the paradox of democratic will-formation has frequently been negotiated (or sublimated) by a "dialectic," in which the conditions necessary for a future democracy are to be established by an exclusive faction of "radical democrats" whose ends justify undemocratic means.[13] Thus, for the Jacobins, an "educational dictatorship" was justified by the goal of creating (by force) a population capable of rational discourse. As Schmitt famously argues, moreover, dictatorship and democracy are in principle entirely compatible. Representative democracy always involves a fiction, inasmuch as a part—whether the majority, a qualified elite, or a single ruler—stands in for a whole (constituent power) that is not concretely present. Indeed, he asserts that with the loss of faith in discussion, dictatorship had in fact become a more popular and more "direct" source of democratic identification than parliamentary procedures. "Compared to a democracy that is direct, not only in the technical sense but also in the vital sense, parliament appears an artificial machinery, produced by liberal reasoning, while dictatorial and Caesaristic methods not only can produce the acclamation of the people but can also be a direct expression of democratic substance and power."[14]

Again, while the failures of the alternative (parliament, in this case) were clear enough, the virtues of dictatorship remained to be explained. It is often noted here that in the Weimar constitution, the president was the only figure directly elected by the people as a whole.[15] But how could the dictator be said to serve the will of a people that he shaped virtually without constraint? What "democratic substance" guided his actions? Put another way, where might the will of the people (*pouvoir constituant*) reside prior to their concrete identification, and how was it channeled by the personal decisions of the dictator? Or, more practically, how could executive authority "produce the acclamation of the people" among the splintered groupings of Weimar? That is, how could faith in such a figure be extracted from antagonistic interests, affections, anxieties, and ideas, and attached to power that can then shape the latter into a "public" with coherent beliefs and desires, and how might this be accomplished in such a way that this public appears the very foundation of sovereign authority?

While Schmitt was ostensibly a juridical thinker, his answers to these questions traversed metaphysics, sociology, and aesthetics. At one extreme, constituent power was a secularized version of God's underived power; at another, it issued from an organic culture, or *terrisme*. Thus, Schmitt's politics has been read alternately as theocratic or racist, and his proper stance remains a subject of contention. Others, noting the slippage of terms in his arguments for supralegal authority, accuse him of an "occasional" or instrumental approach to its justification.[16] Yet it is less often asked just how religion or race (or any other sources of political affiliation and antagonism) are placed in the service of authoritarian democracy in a secular, pluralistic society. In Schmitt's Weimar writings, I find a dynamic relationship between political power and social forms, between tradition and innovation, norm and decision, organic traditions and their strategic deployment, that belies straightforwardly racist or theocratic readings. As these writings indicate, the political constitution of a people and their enemies involves the selection, combination, and amplification of attachments and antagonisms of various kinds. In the process of their assembly, furthermore, these components are also modified. The details of this process, however, vary substantially. In particular, I compare three instances in which Schmitt describes such a process, following the course of his Weimar writings: The Catholic "complex of opposites" (*complexio oppositorum*) (1923), the Marxist myth of class struggle (1923), and the polemical opposition of friend and enemy (1932).

While they exhibit common dynamics, these examples also reflect Schmitt's accommodation (albeit with overlapping themes and occasional reversals) to the increasing dislocation of the nation-state by accelerated movements of finance, warfare, and communication, or what is now sum-marized as "globalization." As the substantial relations and differences on which it draws become increasingly delocalized and unstable, the exercise of supralegal power takes on these same characteristics, or, in the familiar but misleading expression, the exception becomes the rule. Furthermore, the transformation in the practice of government in a period of extensive and volatile global relations—requiring flexible and rapid adjustments to changes across the globe—is accompanied by a shift in the nature of legitimacy, whereby an *ethos* of belief grounded in relatively stable cultural and social rituals is supplanted by a more flexible and mobile *pathos* of identification. In the face of a broad set of economic, political, and cultural dislocations, Schmitt struggled to link the personal authority of a supralegal executive to a legitimate source of constituent power, finally reducing democratic repre-sentation to a vague "confidence" (*Vertrauen*) in a virtually unconstrained executive (in *Legality and Legitimacy*, 1932). As I argue, this trajectory chal-lenges us to consider how, or if, we might move beyond such dissimulations without dispensing with democratic aspirations themselves.

Metaphysical Authority

In his early studies of law and politics—sometimes called his Catholic period—Schmitt frames his critique of liberalism in metaphysical terms, linking the liberal notion of a "self-organizing society" to philosophies of immanence, materialism, or "atheism," which he treated as interchange-able. In *Political Romanticism* (1919), Schmitt describes Romanticism as the philosophical perspective of liberalism in a state of disintegration following the disillusionment with rationalism in the aftermath of the French Revolu-tion.[17] Whereas Enlightenment rationalists had repudiated a transcendent God in favor of a mechanistic conception of the natural world, Romanticism was rooted in a subjective "occasionalism."

> As for every genuine explanation, here too the metaphysical formula is the best criterion. Every movement is based, first of all, on a specific characteristic at-titude toward the world, and second, on a specific idea, even if it is not always conscious, of an ultimate authority, an absolute center. The romantic attitude is most clearly characterized by means of a singular concept, that of the *occasio*. This concept can be rendered in terms of ideas such as occasion, opportunity, and perhaps also chance. It acquires its real significance, however, by means of an opposition. It negates the concept of *causa*, in other words, the force of a calculable causality, and thus also every binding norm. It is a disintegrative concept. This is because everything that gives consistency and order to life and

to what takes place—regardless of whether it is the mechanical calculability of the causal, or a purposive or normative nexus—is incompatible with the idea of the merely occasional.[18]

In a world that yielded neither reason nor purpose, the Romantics retreated from a search for universal principles into the play of subjective experience. They found inspiration in a variety of sources, whether the traditions of history or the innocence of childhood. In every case, these ideas were detached from practical contexts and served only as material for poetic constructions. "This variability of political content is not accidental . . . it is deeply rooted in the nature of the romantic, the essence of which is passivity."[19]

For the Romantic, every stimulus served as an occasion for a play of subjective, emotional experience rather than a practical response. The result was an easy adaptation to diverse historical situations or political regimes, whether the revolution or Metternich's "police state." Hence, their political orientations displayed extreme hypocrisies and contradictions, such as an admiration for the French revolution and for Burke at one and the same time.[20] While in some sense apolitical, however, Romanticism was by no means harmless, inasmuch as the same attitude of passivity permeated the liberal state, which became a medium for the play of conflicting forces.[21] In this light, Schmitt interprets the Romantic ideal of endless "conversation" as a reflection of parliamentary "discussion."[22] He thus sees Romanticism as the height of liberal indecision. He singles out Adam Müller as the archetype for these traits, deriding his "feminine and vegetative nature" and his opportunistic adaptation to varying political positions.[23] As we shall see, this was not the only aspect of this complex work that would later appear deeply ironic.[24]

In *Political Romanticism*, Schmitt declares legitimacy "an absolutely unromantic category."[25] In *Political Theology* (1922), he seeks this ostensibly unromantic legitimacy in the metaphysical opponent of the liberal order, namely transcendent personal authority. Once again, he asserts the metaphysical basis of political concepts, going so far as to claim that all political concepts are secularized theological ones, or in his intriguing but unsubstantiated terms, that juristic concepts share a "radically systematic structure" with the "metaphysical image" proper to each epoch.[26] As he had in *Political Romanticism*, however, Schmitt depicts a struggle between two metaphysical images, namely Catholicism and variants of "atheism," the latter appearing this time in the earlier, more politically optimistic guises of Enlightenment Deism as well as in Russian anarchism.[27] The latter two, he claims, shared a benevolent view of human nature as lawful and peaceable or "good."[28]

By contrast, Catholic philosophers of counterrevolution, particularly Juan Donoso Cortés, presumed the material world and human nature are violent, chaotic, or "evil." "Bonald was no less clear about the fundamentally evil instinct of man and recognized the indestructible 'will to power,' as do modern psychologists. But his conception of human nature pales in comparison with the outbursts of Donoso Cortés, whose contempt for man knew no limits."[29] In principle, Schmitt places the question whether an emergency could be entirely avoided beyond the scope of political theory, leaving it to metaphysics or anthropology.[30] However, having lived through the Great War and its aftermath, during which he was a firsthand witness to public violence, Schmitt clearly sympathizes with Cortés's view. Against legal positivists like Kelsen, Schmitt argues that legal norms themselves rely on a lawful or "normal" flow of events, and cease to function when this flow is interrupted. "There exists no norm that is applicable to chaos."[31] Since the fall, the *status quo* is contingency.

Sovereignty, for Schmitt, adjudicates the normal. According to his well-known formulation, "sovereign is he who decides on the exception."[32] However, the sovereign Schmitt describes does more than merely "decide" when to suspend law in critical situations. In such conditions, the sovereign also (re)establishes the concrete conditions in which it can operate. "All law is situational law. The sovereign produces and guarantees the situation in its totality."[33] By implication, the exception cannot itself be situated. Indeed, the exception "cannot be anticipated, nor can one spell out what may take place in such a case."[34] In turn, sovereignty cannot be normatively circumscribed. "Looked at normatively, the decision emanates from nothingness. The legal force of a decision is different from the result of substantiation. Ascription is not achieved with the aid of a norm; it happens the other way around."[35] So described, the sovereign decision resembles an act of divine intervention that introduces grace to an otherwise chaotic or evil world. "The exception in jurisprudence is analogous to the miracle in theology."[36] One could say Schmitt literalizes Weber's "charismatic" authority.[37]

The relation of subjects to sovereign, it would seem, must therefore be one of blind faith. For DeMaistre, "The two words *infallibility* and *sovereignty* were 'perfectly synonymous.'"[38] The precise meaning of Schmitt's secularization thesis, however, is a subject of controversy. Gopal Balakrishnan, for example, describes Schmitt's recourse to theology as a "flight forward into myth."[39] Hans Blumenberg, in different but related terms, describes it as a flight into metaphor. "Political theology is a metaphorical theology."[40] Both accusations leave open the question of just how infallible authority is established in modern, secular society, that is, how its myths or metaphors become effective, or fail. Schmitt himself points to the problem in the final pages of his text, noting that by substituting a secular dictatorship for a divine King, counter-revolutionary philosophers "heightened the moment of the decision to such an extent that the notion of legitimacy, their starting point, was finally dissolved."[41] In *The Crisis of Parliamentary Democracy* (1923) Schmitt retains his theological terms: "A scientific study of democracy must begin with a particular aspect that I have called political theology."[42] In the modern age, the democratic "will of the people" replaces the will of God as that power which establishes and transcends a legal order. Like the king, the people represent a transcendent source of decision opposed by liberal metaphysics.[43] In the case of democracy, the question of sovereignty, "Who decides?" becomes the question of who has the authority to define the general will. But how is the infallible will of the people itself revealed? Or, how is it transferred to the personal authority of the dictator? Can one speak for the people in the same way one speaks for God? Is religion simply a metaphor for secular authority, or a source of its legitimacy? Perhaps both?

A closer look at Rousseau may be helpful here. In *On the Social Contract*, Rousseau formulated the paradox of democratic founding to which so many, including Schmitt, would return. "In order for an emerging people to appreciate the healthy maxims of politics, and follow the fundamental rules of statecraft, the effect would have to become the cause; the social spirit, which should be the result of the institution, would have to preside over the founding of the institution itself; and men would have to be prior to laws what they ought to become by means of laws."[44] As Rousseau argues, the strong cannot be master, at least not "forever," unless obedience is (already) duty.[45] A constitution can only form a general will if it commands the loyalty of the people, that is, if there is already a general will in favor of the constitution. The task of reconciling law and legitimacy falls first to the great legislator who does not merely establish rules to be imposed by force, but changes human nature, making man collective and dependent.[46] But how can one change human nature? In order to gather public support for the constitution, Rousseau argues, the founder of the Republic can appeal neither to force nor reasoning, but must rely on "another order of authority, which can win over without violence and persuade without convincing," namely, religion. That is, he must "subjugate by means of divine authority those who cannot be moved by human prudence."[47] However, as Rousseau recognized, the turn to divine authority and irrational persuasion only displaces the original paradox, for not just anyone can "make the Gods speak or be believed when he declares himself their interpreter."[48] Nor can just anyone successfully claim to speak for the People.[49]

What sort of capacity, then, does the legislator display? Rousseau refers to the "miracle" of the legislator's "great soul?"[50] But of what does this consist, and how does it differ from the power of reason? If we follow Rousseau's earlier claims regarding the sources of the social compact, it would seem the legislator's ability to persuade without force or reason depends upon the resonance of his speech and laws with prevailing customs, affections, and ideas that are not so much formed as they are evoked and channeled. Rousseau writes, "since men cannot engender new forces, but only unite and direct existing ones, they have no other means of self-preservation except to form, by aggregation, a sum of forces that can prevail over the resistance; set them to work by a single motivation; and make them act in concert."[51] The legislator who perceives the passions of men does not know a fixed human nature, but a diverse array of capacities, tendencies, and inclinations shaped by climate, population, and customs; hence the need to govern a small area, in which these factors are relatively stable and perceptible.[52] Religious traditions, in this case, form the material of the legislator's virtuosic orchestration, and, if we follow Hobbes, are themselves formed by the cultivation of "seeds" of anxiety, superstition, and fancy.[53] I choose to name this dynamic relation between latent tendencies or traits traversing individuals, on the one hand, and an ability to recognize new ways to draw out and assemble them, on the other, *the virtual and the virtuosic*.[54] Rousseau's discussion of censorship provides a further illustration. He writes, "Just as the general will is declared by law, the public judgment is declared by censorship."[55] Just as the law depends upon and organizes virtual commonalities, censorship depends for its success on selective appeals to prevailing, if unthematized, sentiments. "The censorial tribunal, far from being the arbiter of the people's opinion, merely declares it, and as soon as this body departs from that opinion, its decisions are useless and ineffective."[56] This declaration, like legislation, works not to form but "to guide [public] judgment."[57] For the most part, censorship maintains a moral order by "preventing opinions from being corrupt" (it cannot form them once these are lost), but "sometimes even by defining them when they are still uncertain."[58] As an instance of the latter, Rousseau mentions the use of seconds in duels, which, "carried to a mad extreme in the kingdom of France, was abolished by these simple words in an edict of the King: 'As for those who have the cowardice to appoint seconds.' This judgment, anticipating that of the public, determined it at once."[59] Amplified by this declaration, public shame crossed the threshold at which it became decisive. The legislator, likewise, enacts a rule that both "anticipates" and shapes a public judgment. His declaration forms an aperture through which a tendency becomes an actuality.

To rephrase our questions above in this light, in which religious or secular sources did Schmitt find grounds for supra-legal authority in Weimar, and how were they united and directed?

In 1923, the same year he would publish *The Crisis of Parliamentary Democracy*, Schmitt published a short work exploring Roman Catholicism as a source of "political form."[60] At the time, the Catholic Center Party (*Zentrum*) was the only alternative to interest-based or radical parties of either pole, appealing—as its name implied—to a broad range of social positions.[61] Schmitt's explanation for the integrative capacity of the Church centered on an intriguing notion, "*complexio oppositorum*" (complex or combination of opposites), whose exposition aptly illustrates some of the complications of his thinking throughout the period. He clearly derives the phrase from "*coincidentia oppositorum*," used by Nicholas of Cusa to describe the divine enfolding of differences and oppositions.[62] A coincidence of opposites does not involve a rational or logical mediation, but a kind of catechretic unity whereby diverse individuals and qualities remain copresent in God.[63] Schmitt attributes an analogous function to the Catholic Church, which could "represent" diverse values and positions at different times while maintaining an overarching unity. Citing Byron's description of Rome, Schmitt ascribes this ability to the Church's "hermaphroditic nature."[64] "[The Church's] history knows examples of astounding accommodation as well as stubborn intransigence, the manly ability to resist and womanly compliance—a curious mixture of arrogance and humility."[65] Its epicene composition could be embraced by those of diverse orientations, from the authoritarian (Donoso Cortés) to the radical (Padraic Pearse).

According to Schmitt, the Church's *complexio* reflects a combination of (sexual) differences that obtains throughout psychic and social reality:

> The union of antitheses extends to the ultimate socio-psychological roots of human motives and perceptions. The pope is called the Father; the Church is the Mother of Believers and the Bride of Christ. This is a marvelous union of the patriarchal and the matriarchal, able to direct both streams of the most elemental complexes and instincts—respect for the father and love for the mother—toward Rome. Has there ever been a revolt against the mother? Ultimately, most important is that this limitless ambiguity combines with the most precise dogmatism and a will to decision as it culminates in the doctrine of papal infallibility.[66]

Much as Freud mapped psychic structures onto the sexual matrix of the heterosexual family, Schmitt identifies a parallel conflation of sexual difference in both social and psychic complexes. Both the individual psyche and the nuclear family comprise a *complexio oppositorum*, a supple unity consisting of a vague but intense combination of multiple associations that can infuse any number of concrete forms. The Church at once reiterates and channels these complexes—including the organization of instincts in the matrix of sexual difference—giving their force an institutional structure and vice versa.

Whereas the sovereign decision described in *Political Theology* was figured as an "ungrounded ground," the infallible authority Schmitt describes in this text draws on a plurality of attachments, channeled and dissolved in a "stream" that culminates in a fund of legitimate authority (a metaphor of confluence that recurs, as we will see). Rather than imposing form on a chaotic or "evil" nature, the Catholic doctrine Schmitt describes here draws on and consolidates various social and psychological assemblages. Catholicism, he explains, treats human nature as neither wholly good nor evil, but "only weakened and troubled, thus permitting the use of some gradations and adaptations."[67] The Church plays the role of the *Katechon*, or "restrainer," maintaining a worldly order and so holding off the apocalypse.[68] Binary alternatives, Schmitt claims, are foreign to Catholic thought generally, in which matter and spirit, form and content are not opposites in need of a "third" reconciliation.[69] Catholicism refused the modern alternatives of Protestantism, which opposed urbanism, technology, and market rationality to a radically asocial or romantic conception of "wild" nature.[70] The juridical order of the Church was grounded in a synthesis of nature and culture or *"terrisme"* that Schmitt attributes not only to agricultural traditions but also to what he describes as humanistic modes of urbanization that unite "intellect and feeling, or heart; human labor and organic development, nature and reason."[71]

Still linked to a set of instincts and sentiments cultivated by various customs and institutions, Catholic authority could be distinguished from the modern forms of legitimacy outlined by Weber. Schmitt declares its Roman rationalism was neither charismatic nor "impersonal."[72] "The Pope is not a prophet, but the Vicar of Christ. Such a ceremonial function precludes all the fanatical excesses of an unbridled prophetism."[73] Nor is the pope a "commissar" in the Republican vein. His authority remains personal. What this leaves of Weber's categories, of course, is traditional authority, or routinized ("ceremonial") charisma.[74] Indeed, Schmitt explicitly grounds metaphysical authority in a worldly tradition. "No political system can survive even a generation with only naked techniques of holding power. To the political belongs the idea, because there is no politics without authority and no authority without an *ethos* of belief."[75]

So much for a decision that "emanates from nothingness." In this text, the hollowness of abstract norms and the vacuum of legitimacy left by the

secularization of dictatorship in *Political Theology* are filled with beliefs channeled from a variety of religious and cultural institutions. But how is this
channeling accomplished? Just what is the relationship between idea, ethos,
and authority? Although he grounded spiritual authority in a prior ethos,
Schmitt makes no concession to immanence or a self-organizing community. He ultimately traces the "representative power" of the Church back to
the figure of Christ, the visible representative of the invisible, spiritual, or
transcendent.[76] "So long as even the ghost of an idea exists, so also does the
notion that something preceded the given reality of material things—that
there is something transcendent—and this always means an authority from
above. To a type of thinking which derives its norms from the economic-
technical sphere, this appears as an outside interference, a disturbance of
the self-propelling machine."[77] Or, in the more poetic phrasing of his earlier
essay, *The Visibility of the Church* (1917), "life is not a mushroom growing
out of death."[78] Instead, the "lawfulness of the visible world" and the ethical character of human action—which, if it is to be represented, must participate in the spiritual realm—flows from a continuous animation by the
spiritual power of God. The Church oversees this process, instituting a series
of "mediations" of spirit, law, and the social order, of which marriage is the
privileged example.

> Marriage . . . has become the foundation of an allegory whose most profound
> significance lies in that all its components are consecrated—that the woman
> conduct herself toward the man as the man toward his Church, and as the
> Church toward Christ the mediator. It presents a whole hierarchy of media-
> tion, the ground of which is none other than the Word of God. The consolida-
> tion of these relations as legal relations, the transition to the firmer foundation
> which religiosity obtains in the framework of the Church, as love in marriage,
> the limitation of the pneumatic in the juridical, also follow the rhythm of the
> origin of the visible in the invisible God. . . . . The idea obtains its visibility
> in the Word, just as a breath of air becomes a sound when it is forced through
> a reed.[79]

Schmitt's remarkable depiction of this series of mediations conforms to
Catholic doctrine[80] and the medieval logic of a "graduated" universe in which
the opposition of the sensible and intelligible (love and respect) is resolved
by a continuous path of redemption.[81] The institution of the Church is the
culmination of a series of mediations that give rise to the ethos on which
its authority depends. Far from being the sole guarantor of a normal order,
the authority of the leader is the beneficiary of beliefs and desires shaped in
broader institutions. Schmitt goes so far as to claim that if the antichrist were

Pope, "true believers would remain even then the visible Church, would hold to the unbroken chain of the imitation of Christ in the priestly, educational and pastoral offices in a visible, that is, juridical continuity."[82]

This unfolding of the invisible into the visible is not a betrayal, or "hypocrisy" as it is for Protestantism, because the material world is not wholly evil. Spirit can be expressed through the Church, which is not only in but also "of" the world. One is tempted to call Schmitt's conception of the juridical "transubstantiational." Yet in *Roman Catholicism and Political Form*, Schmitt does more than mystify law and authority—or draw theological analogies. He also describes rhetorical and iconographic practices by which the mystical Idea is represented in the material world. The Catholic Idea, he explains, was communicated especially in *aesthetic* traditions of art, dress, music, and architecture. "What first strikes the attention of an age devoted to artistic enjoyment is that which is last in natural and historical development—the crowning fulfillment and ultimate gift, the aesthetic beauty of form. Form, figure, and visual symbolism arise independently from great representation."[83] As this passage indicates, the aesthetic consolidation of a visible Idea culminates a long process of mediation. It draws on an ethos consecrated (spiritualized) in a variety of institutions and rituals. In an age of technology, this link is broken, and the traditional representative function of aesthetics gives way to "enjoyment." Schmitt laments the broken link between art and religion in the modern age, but suggests, "with respect to the Church, it is not an incurable illness."[84] While the Church may have lost its association with the "creative arts," the power of the Idea ultimately derives from the sensuous power of speech. "The ability to create form, which is essential to aesthetics, has its essence in the ability to create the language of a great rhetoric."[85] A great rhetoric, in turn, consists of a discursive combination of opposites: "Most decisive however, is rhetoric in the sense of what one might call representative discourse, rather than discussion and debate. It moves in antitheses. But these are not contradictions; they are the various and sundry elements molded into a *complexio* and thus give life to discourse."[86]

It would appear the mystical power of representation circulates in everyday language, waiting to be channeled by anyone capable of virtuosic rhetoric, or "representative discourse." However, in typical fashion, Schmitt insists the vital force of rhetoric "presupposes a hierarchy, because the spiritual resonance of great oratory derives from the belief in the representation claimed by the orator."[87] Indeed, "the idea of representation is so completely governed by conceptions of personal authority that the representative as well as the person represented must maintain a personal dignity—it is not a materialist concept."[88] A personal representative has "dignity" (*Würde*), we have seen, insofar as he or she is the bearer of a spiritual Idea, rather than venal (material) interests. However, as Schmitt also suggests, the link between the spiritual idea and the worldly authority of a representative figure is sustained by an ethos of belief (in this case, belief in the representative status of the orator). This belief, in turn, is organized in aesthetic and discursive traditions, just the dignity of a representative is sustained not only by titles but style and comportment, even physiognomy (*die Würde* can also signify "portliness"). It is by virtue of their participation in these traditions that the members of the Church participate in the invisible realm represented by the visible figures of the Church. "The Catholic Church is the sole surviving contemporary example of the medieval capacity to create representative figures—the pope, the emperor, the monk, the knight, the merchant."[89]

Schmitt's account of the *complexio oppositorum* is thus itself a combination of "opposites," traversing psychological, aesthetic/rhetorical, and personal perspectives. It describes a psychic fusion of emotive attachments, the symbolic or rhetorical reproduction of such fusion, and its personification in a "representative" figure. Logically, these different moments form a circle. Authority requires an ethos of belief, which requires an Idea formed by "representative discourse" that, in turn, requires the authority of a speaker, and so on. However, by unfolding the mutual dependence of authority and form (or decision and norm) in a temporal process, Schmitt reveals the diverse practices through which the power of the invisible idea is drawn from the dispersion of the visible world, and by which the political "paradox" is negotiated, namely though a continuous relay between a plurality of traditions in which habits, ideas, and affections are shaped and their strategic appropriation or refiguring. In this process, the choice between immanent and transcendent perspectives becomes almost a quibble. If we prefer to invert the priority of matter and spirit, or idea and representation, we merely enter at a different juncture.

As a complex of opposites, the Catholic Church could accommodate a variety of political positions in a continuous tradition of representation.[90] Borrowing an analogy from Cusa, we could compare the visible unity of the Church to that of a portrait whose gaze follows you as you move about it, and does likewise for an indefinite number of viewers, tracking them even as they move about and change positions.[91] Without becoming substantially equivalent, every group and individual could be represented in the Church, inasmuch as they already participate in the invisible realm represented by its visible figure. In the same vein, Schmitt hoped to incorporate the competing forces of Weimar in an encompassing legal order.

In the social world, secular jurisprudence also manifests a certain *complexio* of competing interests and tendencies. Like Catholicism, it also evidences a curious mixture of traditional conservatism and revolutionary resistance in line with natural law . . . jurisprudence can easily assume a posture similar to Catholicism with respect to alternating political forms in that it can positively align itself with various and sundry power complexes, provided only there is a sufficient minimum of form to "establish order."[92]

Schmitt extends the notion of the *complexio* to secular jurisprudence, which includes not only positive laws but also flexible sources of legitimacy. As we will see, he would later argue that an executive might act as an agent of law broadly conceived, a "visible" representative who suspends positive statutes and rules by decisions that nonetheless carry a minimum of form.[93] As Schmitt saw it, the Church would not replace but supplement secular representation, infusing secular power with a "living idea." However, he identified the capacity for flexible alliances and complex combinations with any movement possessed of a "definite world outlook" or "ultimate principle." "From the standpoint of a world-view, all political forms and possibilities become nothing more than tools for the realization of an Idea."[94]

Schmitt's position in relation to this standpoint remains a subject of contention. One might say it looks different depending upon the point at which one enters the triangular relationship between authority, idea, and representative practice. Joseph Bendersky reads Schmitt's text as "nothing less than a reaffirmation of his allegiance to the Church."[95] Jan-Werner Müller, by contrast, sees in it an attempt to "instrumentalize" religion.[96] More broadly, Ellen Kennedy finds a division throughout Schmitt's thought between constructive fictions and search for higher truth. As she puts it, "he is torn between decisionist and normative theory."[97] Ultimately, she claims he internalized the spiritual logic described in *The Visible Church*, making him "fatally susceptible finally to 'the myth of the state.'"[98] However, Schmitt's analysis of the complex of opposites and the mutual dependence of power, ideas, and ethics does not merely waver between norm and decision, but shows them to be deeply interconnected in an active process whereby a continuous political form is sustained in a temporal unfolding. Regardless of his own faith or lack thereof, Schmitt insisted that political authority must flow from an Idea. It is therefore not wrong to call his view of authority "mystical."[99] However, the integrating force of the Idea is predicated on the shaping and channeling of sentiments, ideas, and habits—including belief, love, respect, admiration, and fear—in an array of prepolitical institutions. The "force of law" carried by executive decisions is extracted from these extra-legal sources through a series of symbolic and rhetorical traditions.

As these traditions give way, however, the mystical power of representation is threatened. This danger finds expression in Schmitt's discussion of the "*Arcanum*":

> The eighteenth century staked much on self-confidence and the aristocratic concept of secrecy. In a society that no longer has such courage, there can be no more "arcane," no more hierarchy, nor more secret diplomacy, in fact, no more politics. To every great politics belongs the "*arcanum*." Everything will take place on stage (before an audience of papagenos).[100]

Secrecy indicates a sphere of authority above the play of positive (visible) interests. This reserve was always implied by the visible Idea of the Church, which, as Derrida said of Augustine, maintained the power of the "secret" even when acting "in its name."[101] The same courage was required to negotiate the "dialectical" dimension of the democratic project, shaping a substantive popular will in the name of its not-yet-visible future. As we saw above, humanism began with this courage (depicted in Mozart's *Magic Flute*), imposing a "dictatorship of reason" against economically defined interests. Ultimately, however, positive interests triumphed over Reason, leaving democratic representation without substance. Schmitt compares the manipulation of power by the Roman priest to that of Dostoyevsky's Grand Inquisitor. Against Dostoyevsky's "fundamentally anarchistic—and that always means atheistic" rejection of such power, Schmitt insists, "Only in God is the conflict between power and good ultimately resolved. But the desire to escape this conflict by rejecting every earthly power would lead to the worst inhumanity."[102]

With the decline of the Church, where else might an Idea be found? On what beliefs and traditions could the mystical power of democratic representation be based? How can such authority serve as a model in a modern, secular society? Or, returning to Rousseau's terms, what other forces might be "united and directed"? George Schwab sees Schmitt's preference for traditional rather than charismatic authority in "contradiction" with the practice of charismatic politics by the groups he supported.[103] As I will argue, however, Schmitt's subsequent formulation of secular authority complicates Weber's distinction between traditional and charismatic authority. Secular charisma, it shows, also rests on a channeling of diverse cultural resources, though both these resources and the tactics of their political articulation are transformed.

Notes

1. Carl Schmitt, *The Crisis of Parliamentary Democracy*, trans. Ellen Kennedy (Cambridge, MA: MIT Press, 1988), hereafter, *CPD*.

2. Schmitt, *CPD*, 21.

3. Schmitt, *CPD*, 24.

4. Schmitt, *Der Huter der Verfassung*. Archiv des offentlichen Rechts, Neue Folge, XVI (March 1929), 161–237. Cited in Joseph Bendersky, *Carl Schmitt, Theorist for the Reich* (Princeton, NJ: Princeton University Press, 1983), 113.

5. Cf. Carl Schmitt-Doroti, *Die Diktatur* (Munchen: Duncker & Humblot, 1921).

6. Schmitt-Doroti, *Die Diktatur*, 136.

7. Schmitt-Doroti, *Die Diktatur*, x. Cf. George Schwab, *The Challenge of the Exception* (Berlin: Dunker & Humblot, 1970), 33–34.

8. See, for example, Giorgio Agamben, *State of Exception*, 34.

9. Schmitt, *CPD*, 9.

10. Schmitt, *CPD*, 26–27.

11. Carl Schmitt, *Verfassungslehre* (Berlin: Duncker & Humblot, 1989). The relationship between constitutional and constituent power will be discussed in greater detail.

12. Schmitt, *CPD*, 29.

13. Schmitt, *CPD*, 2.

14. Schmitt, *CPD*, 17.

15. See Bendersky, *Carl Schmitt*, 112.

16. See, for example, Jan-Werner Müller, *A Dangerous Mind* (New Haven, CT: Yale University Press, 2003).

17. For Oakes's assessment, see his introduction to Carl Schmitt, *Political Romanticism*, trans. Guy Oakes (Cambridge, MA: MIT Press, 1986), xxxv, fn. 26, hereafter, *PR*.

18. Schmitt, *PR*, 16–17.

19. Schmitt, *PR*, 115.

20. Schmitt, *PR*, 131.

21. Schmitt, *PR*, 122.

22. Schmitt, *PR*, 139.

23. Schmitt, *PR*, 128.

24. See Bendersky, *Carl Schmitt*, 27.

25. Schmitt, *PR*, 124.

26. Carl Schmitt, *Political Theology*, trans. George Schwab (Cambridge, MA: MIT Press, 1988), 45–46, hereafter cited as *PT*.

27. Schmitt, *PT*, 50.

28. Schmitt, *PT*, 55.

29. Schmitt, *PT*, 58.

30. Schmitt, *PT*, 7.

31. Schmitt, *PT*, 13.

32. Schmitt, *PT*, 5.

33. Schmitt, *PT*, 13.

34. Schmitt, *PT*, 6. Or, as Jurgen Habermas more delicately puts it, "It is not easy to determine empirically the probability of boundary conditions under which the possible crisis tendencies actually set in and prevail." Habermas, *Legitimation Crisis* (Boston: Beacon Press, 1975), 33.

35. Schmitt, *PT*, 31–32.

36. Schmitt, *PT*, 36.

37. Cf. Max Weber, "The Types of Legitimate Domination," in *Economy and Society* (Berkeley: University of California Press, 1978), 216: "The concept of 'Charisma' ("gift of grace") is taken from the vocabulary of early Christianity."

38. Schmitt, *PT*, 55.

39. Gopal Balakrishnan, *The Enemy* (New York: Verso, 2000), 47.

40. Hans Blumenberg, *The Legitimacy of the Modern Age* (Cambridge, MA: MIT Press, 1983), 101.

41. Schmitt, *PT*, 65.

42. Schmitt, *CPD*, 32.

43. See Schmitt, *PT*, 61.

44. Jean-Jacques Rousseau, *On the Social Contract*, trans. Judith Masters (New York: St. Martin's Press, 1978), 69.

45. Rousseau, *On the Social Contract*, 48.

46. Rousseau, *On the Social Contract*, 68.

47. Rousseau, *On the Social Contract*, 69–70.

48. Rousseau, *On the Social Contract*, 70.

49. As he also argues, a legislator must inherit a people already suited to good laws. Cf. Rousseau, *On the Social Contract*, 72.

50. Rousseau, *On the Social Contract*, 70.

51. Rousseau, *On the Social Contract*, 52–53.

52. See Rousseau, *On the Social Contract*, 72.

53. See Thomas Hobbes, *Leviathan* (Oxford: Oxford University Press, 1998), chapter 11.

54. The latter is a provisional title for a work in progress.

55. Rousseau, *On the Social Contract*, 123.

56. Rousseau, *On the Social Contract*, 123.

57. Rousseau, *On the Social Contract*, 124.

58. Rousseau, *On the Social Contract*, 124.

59. Rousseau, *On the Social Contract*, 124.

60. Carl Schmitt, *Römischer Katholizismus und politische Form* (Stuttgart: Klett-Cotta, 1984), hereafter *RK*; Schmitt, *Roman Catholicism and Political Form*, trans. G. L. Ulmen (Westport, CT: Greenwood Press, 1996), hereafter *RCPF*. Schmitt was himself a Catholic, and at the time, the Catholic Center party was the only popular alternative

to either Communists or Fascists. However, while Schmitt clearly identified with the Church, he was not a member of the *Zentrum*. Cf. Bendersky, *Carl Schmitt*, 15.

61. Weber singles out the *Zentrum* in this respect. Cf. Weber, "The Types of Legitimate Domination," *Economy and Society*, 287.

62. See Nicholas of Cusa, *The Vision of God*, trans. Emma Gurney Salter (New York: Frederick Unger Publishing Co., 1960), 47: "For thou art where speech, sight, and understanding are the same, and where seeing is one with being seen, and hearing with being heard, and tasting with being tasted, and touching with being touched, and speaking with hearing, and creating with speaking."

63. See Ernst Cassirer, *The Individual and the Cosmos*, trans. Mario Domandi (New York: Dover, 2000).

64. Schmitt, *RCPF*, 5.

65. Schmitt, *RCPF*, 5.

66. Schmitt, *RCPF*, 8.

67. Schmitt, *RCPF*, 8. Compare Schmitt's description of the view of eighteenth- and nineteenth-century liberal thinkers who imagined human nature as "rough, but educable." Schmitt, *PT*, 56.

68. The significance of this figure will be discussed further below.

69. Schmitt, *RCPF*, 11. Schmitt thus rejected the relegation of Catholicism to the status of a "hygienic institution for enduring the rigors of competition, a Sunday outing or a summer sojourn of big-city dwellers." Cf. Schmitt, *RCPF*, 12.

70. Schmitt, *RCPF*, 10.

71. Schmitt, *RCPF*, 10–11.

72. See also Schmitt, *PR*, 6, where Schmitt distinguished Catholicism's moral order from either rationalism or romanticism.

73. Schmitt, *RCPF*, 14.

74. George Schwab describes Schmitt as choosing this alternative. See Schwab, *Challenge*, 125.

75. Schmitt, *RCPF*, 17.

76. Schmitt, *RCPF*, 19.

77. Schmitt, *RCPF*, 27.

78. Carl Schmitt, "The Visibility of the Church," trans. G. L. Ulmen, appendix to *RCPF*, 56.

79. Schmitt, "The Visibility of the Church," 57.

80. See Karl Rahner and Herbert Vorgrimler, *Theological Dictionary*, ed. Cornelius Ernst, trans. Richard Strachan (New York: Herder and Herder, 1965), 80–81.

81. See Cassirer, *The Individual and the Cosmos*, 9. Cf. Cassirer, *The Individual and the Cosmos*, 18: "Through the miracle of the ecclesiastical order of life and salvation, transcendence was now both recognized and conquered. In this miracle, the invisible had become visible, the inconceivable had become conceivable to man."

82. Schmitt, "The Visibility of the Church," 55. Kantorowitz explores the extension of this continuum to the "Christological" King. Cf. Kantorowitz, *The King's Two*

Bodies: A Study in Medieval Political Theology (Princeton, NJ: Princeton University Press, 1957).

83. Schmitt, *RCPF*, 22.

84. Schmitt, *RCPF*, 23.

85. Schmitt, *RCPF*, 22.

86. Schmitt, *RCPF*, 23. Cf. *RK*, 39–40.

87. Schmitt, *RCPF*, 24.

88. Schmitt, *RCPF*, 21; *RK*, 35–36.

89. Schmitt, *RCPF*, 19.

90. See Cassirer, *The Individual and the Cosmos*, 30.

91. See Cusa, *Vision of God*, 42; Cassirer, *The Individual and the Cosmos*, 32.

92. Schmitt, *RCPF*, 29–30. Clearly, the legal idea is not equivalent to a self-enclosed system of positive law. Thus, Schmitt can speak of "faith" in the constitution and in legal process.

93. We will explore this further with regards to Schmitt's *Verfassungslehre* and *Legality and Legitimacy*. Cf. Agamben, *Exception*, 33. See also 37–38 on law as "floating signifier."

94. Schmitt, *RCPF*, 5; *RK*, 9.

95. Bendersky, *Carl Schmitt*, 48.

96. Jan-Werner Müller, *A Dangerous Mind*, 23.

97. Ellen Kennedy, *Constitutional Failure, Carl Schmitt in Weimar* (Durham, NC: Duke University Press, 2004), 71.

98. Kennedy, *Constitutional Failure*, 76.

99. See Agamben, *Exception*, 39.

100. Schmitt, *RCPF*, 34. See also Ulmen, "Introduction," Schmitt, *RCPF*, xxiii. See also Schmitt, *CPD*, 37, in which he explains that secrecy is properly illegitimate in an institution based on open discussion and "public opinion."

101. Jacques Derrida, "Passions," in David Wood, ed. *Derrida: A Critical Reader* (Cambridge, UK: Blackwell, 1992), 21.

102. Schmitt, *RCPF*, 32.

103. Schwab, *Challenge*, 125.

CHAPTER THREE

~

From Ethos to Pathos

Myth and Substance

In *Roman Catholicism and Political Form*, Schmitt still saw in Parliament some
remainder of formative authority (granting it the "theoretical" status of a
complex of opposites), over and above the competing instructions of individuals and parties.[1] "The simple meaning of the principle of representation
is that the members of parliament are representatives of the whole people
and thus have an independent authority *vis-à-vis* the voters."[2] Parliament
had initially been conceived to serve the common good of the people as a
whole, comprehended through rational discussion, rather than a plurality
of interests. This was the basis of the economic critique of the Marxists, for
which Schmitt reserved most of his disdain. For the Bolsheviks, "the 'whole'
of the people is only an idea; the whole of the economic process, a reality."[3]
Yet without the capacity to abstract from concrete difference, there can be
no integrating representation. "No great social antithesis can be solved by
economics. . . . It concerns the ethical or legal determination of who is actually the producer, the creator, and therefore the owner of modern wealth."[4]
Schmitt acknowledged Auguste Comte's attempt to elevate modern personae
(the savant or merchant) to the level of representative types but found the
results "embarrassing."[5] In economic discourse, the complex of opposites
proper to representation gave way to "technical" definitions of identity
and interest. "The logical outcome was the class-concept of the proletariat,
which groups society materialistically—according to one's position in the
process of production—and thus conforms to economic thinking. Thereby

it demonstrates that the renunciation of every representation is inherent in this type of thinking."[6]

In *The Crisis of Parliamentary Democracy*—published later the same year (1923)—the representational status of Parliamentarism and Marxism is effectively reversed. Schmitt describes the former, as we have seen, as a forum for competing particular interests. At the same time, he traces the transformation of Marxism from an economic theory to a vital political myth, distinguishing rationalist and irrationalist variants. He finds the latter exemplified by Georges Sorel's conception of the "myth" of the General Strike. In this text, such myths effectively replace the *complexio oppositorum* as alternatives to an "objective" representation of interests. As Sorel argued, a myth is not a description of a given political situation, but a force that acts from within it, a mobilizing self-understanding that emerges spontaneously in the course of revolutionary praxis.[7] Schmitt interprets Marx's critical writings from this perspective, drawing out their messianic and polemical significance. While Marx inherited Hegel's teleological model of history, Marxists were for the most part not content simply to wait for the arrival of Communism. For those seeking an active role in a prescribed sequence of events, the question became how to know when the historical signal for their action has been given, that is, when the time for an overturning of all previously existing social relations has arrived. A productive tautology emerged at this point, whereby, as was the case for Hegel, consciousness of historical *telos* heralded its culmination.[8]

Schmitt thus reads Marx's exhaustive analysis of bourgeois economies as a "demoniacal" Hegelian compulsion to display the consciousness that signals an imminent historical rupture. However, he argues that rather than his technical analysis of capitalism, Marx's genuine political contribution was his synthesis of complex economic struggles in a polemical opposition of labor and capital. "The contradictions of many classes were thus simplified into a single, final contradiction. . . . This simplification signified a powerful increase in intensity."[9] We might add that Marx himself affirmed a combination of representation and intensification in class struggle. "No class in civil society can play this part [emancipating itself and in so doing emancipating society as a whole] unless it can rouse, in itself and in the masses, a moment of enthusiasm in which it associates and mingles with society at large, identifies with it, and is felt and recognized as the *general representative* of this society."[10] As Schmitt explains, the Marxist unification of diverse struggles was achieved by a world outlook concentrated in a powerful "image" [*Bild*] of the bourgeois enemy and linked to a messianic historical mission. This image arose from the combined energies of a variety of antagonisms. Schmitt traces the gathering of resentment toward the bourgeoisie across both territories and genres, from French aristocratic disdain and aesthetic contempt (that of Baudelaire in particular) to the scientific-evolutionary condemnation of Marx and Engels. "All the energies that had created this image were united on Russian soil. Both the Russian and the Proletarian saw now in the bourgeois the incarnation of everything that sought to enslave life's art in a deadly mechanism."[11] Thus, Marxism becomes politically effective precisely when it loses its practical specificity. Class conflict becomes a mobilizing (messianic) myth, elevated above the tawdry, finite goals and limited achievements of objective struggles.

> The Great psychological and historical meaning of the social theory of myth cannot be denied. And the construction of the bourgeois by means of Hegelian Dialectic has served to create an image of the enemy that was capable of accumulating all the emotions of hatred and contempt. I believe that the history of this image of the bourgeois is just as important as the history of the bourgeoisie itself.[12]

Schmitt found the political potentials of Marxist doctrine realized by Lenin, who rejected economistic reductions of political motives to objective class positions. As Lenin saw, class struggle produced many local antagonisms, but they had to be unified and given political significance by Marxist doctrine and leadership. He argued that the economism of trade unionism and the terrorism of the anarchists rested on a similarly misguided faith in spontaneity. Anarchists used terror as means to "excite" workers, provoking a rupture of conventions and an opportunity for spontaneous reorganization. However, as Lenin pointed out, a great deal of excitement and tension already circulated within the conventional order. Everyday life was replete with outrage at great crimes and a multiplicity of "social evils," "but we are unable to gather, if one may so put it, and concentrate all these drops and streamlets of popular resentment that are brought forth to a far larger extent than we imagine by the conditions of Russian life, and that must be combined into a single gigantic torrent."[13]

Schmitt would later herald Lenin for his insights regarding the polemical basis of politics.[14] As both understood, the problem was not the creation of antagonism but its concentration and channeling. This was achieved not in a single stroke, but through a series of contributing actions, culminating in a powerful image of class war. As it migrated eastward, however, the image of the bourgeois became increasingly associated with national as well as class antagonisms. Ultimately, as Schmitt argues, the former would win out. "The more naturalistic conceptions of race and descent, the apparently more typical *terrisme* of the Celtic and romance peoples, the speech, tradition, and consciousness of a shared culture and education, the awareness of belonging to a community with a common fate or destiny, a sensibility of being different from other nations—all of that tends toward a national rather than a class consciousness today."[15] Schmitt's description of the image of the bourgeois enemy conforms in many respects with his description of the *complexio oppositorum*.[16] In particular, it recalls the image of the Catholic Church framed by its enemies. "With its mythic force, this image has had a more profound and powerful effect than any economic calculation."[17] Once again, a confluence of sentiments becomes the basis for a unification of diverse groupings in a visible figure. By adopting Sorel's theory of myth, however, Schmitt effectively acknowledges the synthetic character of "representative" images. Rather than a stable matrix of cultural traditions, the "representative" image of the bourgeois channels shifting (my) themes dispersed across different regions and genres. We can read this shift from *complexio* to myth as an indication of the increasingly mobile and artificial character of political symbols and values in an age of accelerated technological and social change. As indicated by the modern connotation of "myth," social form appears more an instrument rather than a foundation of political agency and authority.

However, for Schmitt, the synthetic character of myth does not make it a mere artifact of power. A myth still draws on a set of substantial traits, even if *terrisme* has become increasingly fluid or mobile. Like a complex of opposites, a myth in some sense "represents" the diverse array of ideas and affections it combines. Given the localizing tendencies of speech, education, and so forth, national complexes have greater resonance than those appealing to a broader class-consciousness. Not all myths are created equal, and (as Benedict Anderson has shown) the nationalist myth thrives on the interplay of imagined and substantial modes of collective life. Or, rather, imagination has its own complex territoriality shaped by the intersection of media technologies, language, economy, and so on.[18]

As we noted above, the extent to which Schmitt understood Catholicism as a driving force or an instrument of political strategy is subject to debate. Regardless, Schmitt's emphasis on nationality and territory signaled a turn away from Catholic rationalism. By the mid-1920s, Schmitt's hope that the Church could contain the plurality of conflicting interests in Weimar within its continuous "juridical" tradition had faded. Eventually, we might say, Schmitt recognized that one can indeed revolt against one's mother, a revolt that in his case coincided closely with excommunication (following his second marriage in 1926).[19]

Politics and Intensity

In *The Concept of the Political* (1927, revised 1932), Schmitt abandons theological terms and instead takes up a formal or "relative" definition of sovereignty.[20] In this text, a political association is defined as such by an ontological or "existential" (*seinsmäßig*) confrontation with an enemy, that is, by one that poses the threat of war.[21] While allowing that any of a number of positive conflicts can combine in and give rise to such a confrontation, whether religious, economic, or ethno-cultural, Schmitt no longer privileged one source of collective affiliation over another. Instead, he described a general logic or process of "the political" as such. Antagonism becomes political or "public" at a crucial *threshold of intensity* beyond which it transcends the normative or ideological distinctions from which it arose.

> The political can derive its energy [*Kraft*] from the most varied human endeavors, from the religious, economic, moral, and other antitheses. It does not describe its own substance, but only the intensity of an association or dissociation of human beings whose motives can be religious, national (in the ethnic or cultural sense), economic, or of another kind and can effect at different times different coalitions and separations. The real friend-enemy grouping is existentially [*seinsmäßige*] so strong and decisive that the nonpolitical antithesis, at precisely the moment at which it becomes political, pushes aside and subordinates its hitherto purely religious, purely economic, purely cultural criteria and motives to the conditions and conclusions of the political situation at hand. In any event, that grouping is always political that orients itself [*sich orientiert*] toward this most extreme possibility.[22]

The political, so understood, can emerge "from every domain."[23] Hence Schmitt rejected the liberal depoliticization of aesthetic, economic, and moral spheres of action. All these realms, while not political as such, harbor intensities that can—if amplified or combined with others—become catalysts for violence. As we saw in the discussion of myth above, for example, class conflicts can resonate with aesthetic or ethnic differences.[24] Like a Myth or a *complexio oppositorum*, the existential antagonism "most of all" draws on a plurality of conflicts, each of which contributes to a fund of *affective* accumulation. "Emotionally the enemy is easily treated as being evil and ugly, because every distinction, most of all the political, as the strongest and most intense of the distinctions and categorizations, draws upon other distinctions for support. This does not alter the autonomy of such distinctions."[25]

The autonomy of the political, as Schmitt describes it, takes a curious form. Rather than having distinct sources, political identification appears out of the amplification or conflation of various nonpolitical distinctions. "Every concrete antagonism becomes that much more political the closer it approaches the most extreme point, that of the friend-enemy grouping."[26] The difference between the politics and other forms of association would seem to be one of degree rather than kind. However, the heightened intensity of political conflict involves not only a change of quantity but also one of quality, just as at a certain temperature and pressure steam undergoes a "phase shift" and becomes water, or water ice, or, if you will, spirit becomes matter. When a conflict becomes political it sheds the "normative" (moral, aesthetic, etc.) distinctions from which it arose. One finds oneself confronted by a minatory other, and it no longer matters how one got to this point. As the intensity of alignments approaches this extreme, the enemy becomes a palimpsest and finally blurs, ultimately losing any recognizable form. At this crucial threshold, conflict is purified of ideological content and becomes properly existential, or political.[27] The political other is not a familiar opponent, a competitor on the same field, but a stranger.[28] In Schmitt's terms, enmity thereby becomes "public," a case of *hostis* rather than *inimicus*. Once this line is crossed, Schmitt claims, accumulated affectively laden oppositions give way to an orientation to physical struggle. Thus, a struggle becomes not only more intense, but different in kind. Indeed, intensity itself, having brought antagonism to this point, bows to the existential perspective it has wrought. Once identified, the public enemy need not be hated, only fought. "A private enemy is a person who hates us, whereas a public enemy is a person who fights against us."[29] Of course, as Clausewitz understood, emotions, both private and public, are hardly irrelevant to fighting, and not likely to disappear.[30]

Contrary to some misconceptions, Schmitt did not identify the political with the practice of war *per se*. "War is neither the aim nor the purpose nor even the very content of politics."[31] Rather, the political character of an entity resides in its capacity to distinguish friend and enemy, that is, the capacity for the *decision* that distinguishes the properly war-inducing situation from the banalities of everyday conflict. "What always matters is the possibility of the extreme case taking place, the real war, and the decision whether this situation has or has not arrived."[32] In principle, the political becomes a limiting criterion for the use of physical violence. Only, how can one know when the situation is at hand? As Schmitt makes clear, there is no objective view of what constitutes an existential threat. "Each participant is in a position to judge whether the adversary intends to negate his opponent's way of life (*seinsmässige Art von Leben*) and therefore must be repulsed or fought in order to preserve one's own form of existence (*Art Existenz*)."[33] Any affiliation and antagonism can potentially become a source of violent struggle. Of course, this does not validate the pluralist critique of sovereignty that emphasizes the many associations that influence social behavior. The latter fails to comprehend the transition described above, in which a plurality of antagonisms fuses in a conflict that transcends them all. The political is always the limit of pluralism, regardless of the plurality of its sources.[34] Where competing associations negate the capacity of anyone to declare war the political is not pluralized but merely (temporarily) suppressed.[35] Once again: "The political entity is by its very nature the decisive entity, regardless of the sources from which it derives its last psychic motives. It exists or it does not exist. If it exists, it is the supreme [höchste], that is, in the decisive case, the authoritative entity."[36]

Although the political so understood may not be eliminated, it becomes difficult if not impossible to locate its proper site. Every grouping not only carries proto-political intensities but can also become a site of decision, and hence sovereign. Nor can one distinguish as political the grouping most relevant for other aspects of life. The entity that establishes the friend-enemy antithesis need not rule other aspects of the lives of its members.[37] It would seem that authority no longer requires an ethos of belief. As his emphasis on intensity above suggests, a given grouping or conflict can become increasingly "political."[38] However, it is by no means clear when, or whether, it will reach the critical point and lead to physical violence, or who will be able to bring about this break. At what threshold will enmity, anxiety, or disappointment become impossible to channel through given norms, and what brings about or restrains the latter's transgression? Schmitt paradoxically describes a group as sovereign that is "oriented" toward the threshold, namely, that at which it first appears as such, but it is unclear just what this would mean. "However one may look at it, in the orientation toward the possible extreme case of an actual battle against a real enemy, the political entity is essential, and it is the decisive entity for the friend-enemy grouping; and in this (and not in any kind of absolutist sense), it is sovereign."[39] It would appear that an orientation to the decision could only be verified retroactively, once a properly political distinction has emerged. Every friend-enemy distinction, we might say, will have been made by the sovereign (decisive) entity it defines. Aggression, we know, is not simply a trait, but a capacity that can be catalyzed by diverse environmental factors. In this light, existential conflicts appear as immanent events that spring from prepolitical conflicts. Along these lines, William Connolly argues, "the sovereign is not . . . he (or she) who first decides there is an exception and then how to resolve it. . . . Sovereign is *that* which decides an exception exists and how to decide it, with the *that* composed of a plurality of forces circulating through and under the positional sovereignty of the official arbitrating body."[40] The decision nonetheless remains a transformative event. As Schmitt describes it in this text it brings about a kind of transcendence from within, an *Aufhebung* of social conflict that simultaneously heightens and transcends a complex process of affective accumulation.

It would seem that in *The Concept of the Political* Schmitt adopts a relativistic theory of sovereignty, inasmuch as he rejects its absolutist definition. Yet his account of the relationship between the political entity and the decision recapitulates the dynamic relationship between substantial and constitutive sources of political identity described above, although both the substantial sources of that identity and the means of their channeling have changed. In *Roman Catholicism and Political Form*, the constituent power of religious authority rested on an "ethos of belief" maintained in stable cultural institutions and practices. In the transition from *complexio oppositorum* to myth, we have seen, a clear source of ritual and authority, with its links to an organic *terrisme*, is dislocated by the migration of ideas and cultural forms, a dislocation famously described by Walter Benjamin.[41] In turn, the symbolic, rhetorical, and strategic channeling of affections or resentments takes on a mobile, synthetic quality. However, as Schmitt suggests, it was still possible to privilege certain modes of affiliation and antagonism. The myth of the nation retained an organic appeal that was transformed into a principle of political affiliation by public acts of articulation. In *The Concept of the Political*, the identification of the people still draws on proto-political intensities, but the latter are increasingly detached from territorial or institutional locations. Whereas the *complexio* or the myth draw on and organize various customs and ideologies, the seemingly empty or formal decision combines and transforms diffuse antagonisms that circulate among various groups and fluctuate in response to a dynamic transnational environment. Correspondingly, the constitutive power of rhetoric previously tied to the authority of the speaker in *Roman Catholicism and Political Form* begins to circulate in the polemical contents of "daily speech."[42] "Terminological questions become thereby highly political. A word or expression can simultaneously be reflex, signal, password, and weapon in a hostile confrontation."[43]

Politics, it would seem, had become a mushroom. Rather than a stable set of traditions or an ethos of belief, friend-enemy distinctions arose out of a volatile intersection of domestic and international economic, social, and ideological conflicts. The state had succumbed to society. In turn, sovereignty itself was delocalized and became a mobile capacity. In the later years of Weimar, this meant nothing less than that the ability to mobilize collective struggle was no longer monopolized by the state. Amidst the numerous financial and political crises facing the Republic, it remained to be seen on what basis and by whom the people would be distinguished from their enemies. Intense forms of association proliferated, with class and party movements challenging the Republic for the status of a "representative" group.[44] At the same time, the sovereignty of the state was jeopardized by the Versailles treaty, which, by hobbling the military capacity of Germany, also threatened its political integrity. Indeed, Ellen Kennedy claims, "Allied hegemony over defeated Germany was the primary source of Weimar's domestic crisis, which the major foreign policy questions of the Republic's middle years intensified."[45] Additionally, as vividly demonstrated by the sudden resurgence of the Nazis after the crash of 1929, international markets had profound effects on the nature and intensity of domestic conflicts.[46]

Capturing the Political:
Constituent Power and Representation

Schmitt, of course, was not yet reconciled to the dislocation of national sovereignty.[47] Even as its cultural, economic, and territorial autonomy was dissolving, the priority of the state remained a constant. He expressed alarm at prospects of civil conflict, and contempt for the banality of everyday "intrigues."[48] Until the capture of the Republic by the Nazis (though hardly a moment later), Schmitt sought to defend the state against the encroachments of radical parties. In short, this meant a defense of the state against Parliament, the channel through which it was flooded by a chaotic society. Between 1924 and 1929, the Republic was in a period of relative stability. In his 1928 *Theory of the Constitution* (*Verfassungslehre*), Schmitt adopts a conservative posture, elevating the constitution above the fray of parliamentary legislation. Whereas the constitution issued from a direct act of self-founding (constituent power) on the part of a unified German people, parliamentary majorities merely cobbled together pluralistic interests and groupings.[49] "The legitimacy of the Weimar constitution is based on the constituent power (*verfassunggebenden Gewalt*) of the German people."[50] Only the people as a whole, therefore, could authorize changes to the constitution's basic structure. In *Legality and Legitimacy* (1932), Schmitt extends democratic legitimacy to the emergency measures of an executive, depicting the latter as a more direct and appropriate form of representative than that of Parliament. Historically, this shift from the "inviolable constitution" to the "*pouvoir neutre*" of its executive guardian corresponded with the transition from the relative normalcy of everyday life in the middle years of the Republic to the resurgence of social crisis and the increasingly frequent use of presidential emergency powers that followed the crash of 1929.[51] Thematically, it described a transition from norm to exception. Across this transition, we have seen, Schmitt draws a continuum. How, then, was the Constitution, and finally the measures of the executive, linked to democratic constituent power?

In a thematically focused essay that synthesizes a "theory of representation" from a combination of Schmitt's Weimar writings, Duncan Kelly outlines tensions associated with Schmitt's attempt to wed Sieyes's notion of democratic constituent power to a Hobbesian personal sovereign. Kelly begins with the "*complexio oppositorum*," noting the spiritual and personal aspects that distinguished Catholic representation from liberalism's economistic or "mechanical" formulations.[52] He finds the same formula at work in the *Verfassungslehre*, where "to represent means to make visible and present an invisible entity through an entity which is publicly present."[53] At stake are the nature of the "invisible entity" and the mode of its public embodiment. In the language Schmitt adopted from Sieyes, the former no longer issues from heaven but from the constituent power ("*pouvoir constituant*") of the people. We thus return to our earlier question, namely, what form do the people take prior to their political articulation, and how does the latter manifest itself as an expression of the former? For Sieyes, constituent power "only appears in the exceptional or extraordinary situation, either in the formation of the nation, or in the selection of "extraordinary" representatives to represent the nation in the Third Estate (Kelly, 125). In the *Verfassungslehre*, Schmitt adopts Sieyes's terms, linking constituent power to the nation.

> During the French revolution Sieyes developed the theory of the people (more precisely: the nation) as the subject of constituent power. . . . Nation and people are often treated as equivalent concepts, however the word "nation" is more succinct and less liable to misunderstanding. Namely, it identifies the people as an entity capable of political action with an awareness of their political distinctness and the will for political existence, whereas a people not existing as a nation is only some kind of ethnically or culturally intertwined, but not necessarily *politically* existing human connection.[54]

The nation is a locus of emotional and ideological identification, one that is then embodied in the positive constitution. The Weimar constitution was understood along these lines as a collective "decision for democracy, that the German people have struck by virtue of their awareness of their political existence as a people."[55]

But how is the unity of the nation composed, prior to its legal constitution? How can the cause of democracy be a democratic decision? Confronting this familiar paradox, Schmitt maintains his earlier claim that democratic identification rests on substantial equality, though "the substance of equality can be different in different democracies and eras."[56] Schmitt explains:

> Various elements can contribute to the unity of a nation and consciousness of that unity: a common language, shared historical destiny, traditions and memories, common political goals and hopes. Language is a very important factor, but not decisive. Decisive is the commonality of historical life, conscious willing of that commonality, great experiences and purposes. Genuine revolutions and victorious wars can overcome linguistic differences and found the feeling of national solidarity, even if the same language is not spoken.[57]

Ellen Kennedy has pointed out commonalities between Schmitt's conception of the nation in *The Concept of the Political* and in the *Verfassungslehre*, describing the latter as a "solution" to dislocation of politics described in the former.[58] In both cases, the homogeneity of a people abides not in concrete similarities *per se* but rather a general consciousness or *feeling* of commonality that is drawn from various sources. While not reducible to an objectively defined set of traits, national identification is nonetheless grounded in substantial relations, whether traditional affiliations, sundry prepolitical associations, or shared transformative experiences. Kelly glosses these complexities when he distinguishes Schmitt's claims for a "substantial" conception of democratic homogeneity—à la Rousseau—from those based on Sieyes's "more abstract" view of the nation as a "politically conscious and unified people."[59]

But again, how does the nation thus conceived express itself, or become an agent of political decisions? For Sieyes, *pouvoir constituant* appeared only at the origin of the constitution, after which the people appear directly as a "*pouvoir commettant*" when choosing representatives.[60] As Schmitt argues, however, modern elections are not characterized by the unified presence of a sovereign demos but a plurality of interests organized by political parties. As Kelly puts it, "the theatrical Hobbesian Leviathan, which held the population in awe, had been transformed by liberalism and capitalism into a simple machine."[61] Schmitt, of course, seeks to renew immediate democratic presence in the figure of the executive. Whereas Sieyes's support for legislative representation was based on a distinction between classical and modern forms of democracy, Schmitt's preference for personal representation—linking the unmediated presence of constituent power to the acts of the sovereign—blurs that distinction. But how could the supralegal acts of the executive at once suspend the constitution and express the will of the people who composed it? Kelly formulates the problem by way of a discussion of Hobbes's Covenant in which—as summarized by Runcimon—"the mutual covenants of the multitude makes 'possible the fiction that they can act as a unity, and commit themselves to the real actions that can maintain that fiction.'"[62] The problem is that in maintaining a fiction (the commonwealth), the sovereign represents an "artificial" being rather than the people, the "natural" source of constituent power. The result is a "circular" logic according to which a sovereign both "represents" and "brings about" the political unity of the people.[63]

We encountered a similar circle in our previous discussion of Rousseau's democratic paradox. There, we saw that prior to their constitution, "the people" is not merely an abstract fiction, but inhabits the multitude as an incipient or virtual convergence of various habits, affections, and ideas. Similarly, representation as Schmitt described it does not merely impose a fictional identity on material multiplicity, but draws on and transforms pre- or protopolitical sources of affiliation and antagonism. Only, how can this be said to obtain for the act of the sovereign? Kelly implies it cannot, drawing a distinction between a people unified as a nation à la Sieyes and the multitude that enters a Hobbesian Covenant. "The modern nation gives form to the people, and hence their constituent power, for the Volk are otherwise understood in democratic theory as an unorganized 'mass' or Hobbesian multitude, capable of making only 'yes or no' acclamatory political decisions."[64] For Schmitt, however,

> The natural form of a people's direct expression of their will is the shout of agreement or disagreement of an assembled crowd, the acclamation. In modern nation-states, the acclamation, which is a natural and necessary life-expression (*Lebensäusserung*) of every people, has changed its form. Here it expresses itself as "public opinion." But the people in general can always only say yes or no, agree or disagree, and their yes or no becomes that much simpler and more elementary the more it concerns a fundamental decision about their own entire existence.[65]

Schmitt cites the Weimar constitution of August 1919 as an example of such a fundamental decision on the part of the people acting through the National Assembly. "Example: The Weimar Constitution of Aug. 11, 1919 (Article 181). 'The German people have agreed on and adopted this constitution through their national assembly. It goes into effect on the day of its announcement.'"[66] For Schmitt, then, the substantial unity of the people is not dissolved when they appear in an acclamatory role. Rather, acclamation indicates a substantial unity, mixing the direct presence of the people with the declarations of representatives.[67] As we saw in Schmitt's discussion of Catholic representation, the multitude already participates in the invisible ("artificial") unity embodied in visible figures of authority. As he wrote in 1923, "The will of the people can be expressed just as well and perhaps better through acclamation, through something taken for granted, an obvious and unchallenged presence, than through the statistical apparatus that has been constructed with such meticulousness in the last fifty years."[68] In acclamations of various kinds, the theatrical presentation of popular unity again takes over from the mechanical representation of interest-based parties.

All that was left was to extend the acclamatory presence of the *Volk* to the emergency measures of the executive. This was achieved once the latter took the form of plebiscites. In this way, the acts of the executive were infused with the immediate presence of constituent power. We can observe some details of this development in Schmitt's account of constitutional and presidential representation in *Legality and Legitimacy*. In this text, the nature of democratic homogeneity changes from a national consciousness shaped by common forms of life and experience to a vague popular "confidence" (*Vertrauen*) in the president. Following my summary of this text, I will inspect the precise nature of this confidence more closely.

Presidential Power and Public Confidence

In the early 1930s, the Republic was unraveling. A global depression, rippling from the collapse of U.S. markets, had devastated the fragile German economy. Radical parties, particularly the Nazis, made rapid gains, and soon challenged the Republic from both inside and out, in the form of antirepublican parliamentary majorities and independent social and militia organizations, respectively. Both activities had led to increasing demands for supralegal authority by both conservatives and liberals. Article 48—the use of which had subsided in the preceding years—was already being used frequently, mainly to manage the economic crisis. In this context, Schmitt sought to legitimate the flexible, rapid measures required for these tasks. In another soon to follow, the same arguments would justify Hitler's consolidation of power. These shifting uses of Schmitt's arguments may be traced in part to the changing mode of legitimacy they articulated. As Schmitt argues, the destabilization of parliamentary legislation led to changes in the relationship between different forms of government that alter their relative popular legitimacy. He finds serious contradictions in the Weimar constitution between various political organs charged with establishing stability in the form of "higher," substantive legal forms that could be protected from volatile parliamentary majorities. The administrative superiority of presidential power stemmed from its greater capacity for rapid responses to shifting situations. However, Schmitt also claims that executive power had a more direct link to a substantial popular will. Thus, he notoriously defends the "legal" status of the decrees issued by a plebiscitary executive.

In *Legality and Legitimacy* (1932), Schmitt reiterates his critique of parliamentary proceduralism.[69] No procedure, he argued, could in and of itself claim legitimacy. Schmitt thus rejected the Weberian notion of "formal" legitimacy of statutes. Rather, a "substantive" basis of law was required to prevent the paradox posed by a rigorous application of the liberal-democratic principle of "equal chance" (Article 25), whereby no group or party could be excluded from legal competition for power.[70] The problem, of course, was that a group could thereby achieve power legally only to use their "political premiums" once in office to eliminate the "equal chance" of others. "The claim to legality renders every rebellion and countermeasure an injustice and a legal violation of illegality. If legality and illegality can be arbitrarily at the disposal of the majority, then the majority can, above all, declare their domestic competitors illegal, that is, *hors-la-loi*, thereby excluding them from the democratic homogeneity of the people."[71] As Schmitt notes, political premiums can be used not only to outlaw other parties, but also indirectly, by its distribution of taxes and public spending, the alteration of elections rules, and so forth, all of which can effectively eliminate the chances of the opposition.[72]

The self-destructive logic of the equal chance for legislative supremacy could be prevented only if the political authority of a parliamentary majority was itself constrained by some form of "higher" values. Indeed, the Weimar constitution had various provisions enumerating substantive rights. However, Schmitt describes such rights as in contradiction with the democratic legitimacy of what he called the "parliamentary legislative state." As he had argued in the *Verfassungslehre*: "Within each political unity, there can be only one subject of constitutional power."[73] The idea that parliamentary statutory law was supreme over all other governmental forms, including basic rights—by virtue of the "legislative reservation"—was enshrined as the highest political power in the first part of the Weimar constitution (esp. Article 68).[74] "In the parliamentary democracy, the will of parliament is identified with that of the people . . . in this regard, a "formal" concept of law is conceivable and acceptable, though not unconditionally formal. It is, instead, entirely connected with the confidence in the congruence between the parliamentary majority and the will of the homogeneous people."[75] By describing such lawmaking as only "conditionally" formal, Schmitt did not mean that it was inspired by substantial values or aims; rather, it was imbued with popular "confidence" (*Vertrauen*), a term to which he links discussions of legitimacy throughout the text.[76] By treating legitimacy as faith, or confidence, Schmitt effectively deprives the link between authority and representation of positive criteria while at the same time treating representation as substantive. As we have seen, confidence has its own historical and material sources. Legal formulations remain blind to these background conditions, whose dissolution had undermined confidence in parliament.

Schmitt suggests that the formal indeterminacy of parliamentary legislation might be "tolerable" under conditions of relatively stable social forms and consolidated property.[77] In "normal" conditions, an otherwise purely formal legal domination preserves the substantive virtues of durable, general legal forms and ensures the trust of minorities that legal opportunities for power would remain open. Under such conditions, confidence is inspired by the predictability of legislative rule, understood to operate within the bounds of a given social, economic, and cultural order. Ultimately, confidence rests on the good faith of others' conventionally circumscribed use of formal political means. In "abnormal" times, however, the "political premium" of legal constituent power becomes "incalculable."[78] Writing in 1932, Schmitt had little need to demonstrate the abnormality of the times, or a lack of public faith in the democratic legitimacy of parliamentary majorities. Not only was parliament composed of irreconcilable factions, but it also had relatively weak links to the administrative state apparatuses, with their potential for purposive or functional legitimacy.[79] Given the sharply divergent aims of these parties, changes in the possession of majority power could lead to severe instability. Electoral processes at the time only compounded the problem. Lists of candidates were assembled by parties in secret, rendering the constitutional language of direct election meaningless. As Schmitt describes them, elections herded masses into "five pens," each of which was defined by irreconcilable principles, policies, and so on. Resorting to metaphors we have encountered several times in this chapter, he writes, "Such a procedure means only that the will of the people will be diverted at the source into five channels and in five different directions, so that it may never flow together in one stream."[80]

Thus, even when transient majorities arose from coalitions of minority factions, the will of the majority remained "heterogeneous."[81] Under these conditions, "The emptiness of mere majority calculus deprives legality of all persuasive power."[82] Loyalty to legal processes was no small matter at the time, when radical parties on both left and right were engaged in armed struggle, and fascist militias substantially outnumbered the German army—explaining Schmitt's repeated references to the problem of the "right of resistance" taken up by minorities with little hope for legal access. Moreover, the properly political will formation of diverse individuals and those processes whereby the Catholic Church had once shaped and captured the affections of its members had been taken over not by the state but by modern "total" parties. "A closer look . . . reveals that we in Germany do not have a total state in fact, but rather a majority of total parties, each of which seeks to achieve the totality in which to entangle their members completely, and attend on people from the cradle to the grave, from nurseries for little children, and on through bowling clubs and sports associations, to funeral and cremation societies . . . and in those ways, fully to politicize people's lives and shatter the unity of the German people."[83] While such problems might have been clear enough at the time, Schmitt takes advantage of the occasion to emphasize the frailty of legal pathos. "The principle of equal chance is of such sensitivity that any serious doubt about the loyalty of all participants already renders the principle's application impossible."[84]

Schmitt saw no "middle road" between what he called the "irreconcilable" principles of the legislative formalism and substantive law, each of which was articulated in different sections of the Weimar constitution.[85] He describes the articles of the "second part" of the Weimar constitution outlining specific protected rights as a "fragment of another type of constitution" or even a "counterconstitution."[86] In particular, he argues that the two-thirds parliamentary majority required to amend the Weimar constitution under Article 76 amounted to a false compromise between two legal principles. The introduction of purely quantitative constraints on majority legislation was not enough, he argues, to compensate for the loss of qualitative confidence in majority representation itself. Only if the majority could be seen also to represent the minority could its superiority be anything other than violent. Echoing the sentiments of J. S. Mill, Schmitt writes, "It would be a peculiar type of 'justice' to declare a majority all the better and more just the more overwhelming it is . . . at this point pure mathematics becomes simple inhumanity."[87] Furthermore, super-majoritarian requirements jeopardized the principles of the parliamentary legislative state properly understood, due to their ability to establish protected measures beyond what Schmitt calls their "appropriate" duration, that is, beyond the momentary presence of a parliamentary expression of democratic will. Yet, at the same time, they failed to establish an extra-legislative sphere of higher law.[88] He describes a law that reflected a pragmatic compromise rather than representing either a present democratic will or absolute values as "senseless, even immoral."[89]

Alongside parliamentary super-majorities, the constitution provided an alternate mode of higher lawmaking by way of direct, plebiscitary democracy in the form of referenda. Once again, Schmitt finds a contradiction, this time within the "first part" of the constitution, whereby two different procedures, each with different principles, could produce the same constitutional transformations. Plebiscites, he notes, had no super-majoritarian requirements, yet in principle represented the same popular will as a parliamentary majority. Schmitt allows that one might consistently establish a "higher law" or a hierarchy of constitutional forms, but they must then be enshrined in distinct political agencies. "There is no hierarchy of norms, but rather only a hierarchy of concrete persons and organs."[90] Establishing "higher" norms therefore had major organizational consequences, leading necessarily to a conflict over which organ held constituent power.[91]

If constituent power appears in the immediate presence of a self-identical democratic will and—as Schmitt had argued in the *Verfassungslehre*—such presence could only take an acclamatory form, it remained only to identify the most proper institutional source of public address. "Plebiscitary legitimacy requires a government or some other authoritarian organ in which one can have confidence that it will pose the correct question in the proper way and not misuse the great power that lies in the posing of the question."[92] The expressive unity of the demos—limited to simple yes or no answers—is thus supplemented with a prior, affective unity, namely confidence in the source of questions. Such confidence, Schmitt allows, can have a variety of objects, whether parliamentary, judicial, or administrative. It could even accrue to the civil bureaucracy, he suggests, though in a limited way. The civil service and the army, in any case, were linked not to parliamentary but to presidential initiatives.[93] The Supreme Court, for its part, could not defend the constitution as a whole.[94] Thus, Schmitt ultimately returns to the presidential emergency powers authorized under Article 48.

When confronted with the obvious objection that the executive, unlike parliament or the judiciary, was not empowered to create law, but only issue decrees or measures, Schmitt essentially reverses the charges. That is, he argues that the difference between statutes and measures had already collapsed in the operation of parliament under abnormal conditions. "The situation is so incalculable and so abnormal that the statutory norm is losing its former character and becoming a mere measure."[95] As an instance of the difference between law and measure, Schmitt cites the distinction between deterrence and retribution. The former deals with concrete factual conditions rather than general principles, and thus is the proper realm of the measure.[96] Measures do not establish norms, but respond to contingent facts and problems in an ongoing fashion. In this respect, Schmitt concludes, "The dictator better conforms to the essence of the administrative state, which manifests itself in the practice of measures, than a parliament that is separated from the executive and whose competence consists in producing general, pre-established and enduring norms."[97] Schmitt attributes the superior administrative virtues of the executive to its capacity to produce both law and the concrete situation in which it applied. Whereas Parliament could only issue decrees, the sovereign could simultaneously undertake whatever action was necessary to produce a normal situation in which they applied. Such actions retained a normative continuity insofar as they were undertaken in the name of "undetermined concepts" like public order.[98] "He unites in himself lawmaking and legal execution and can enforce directly the norms he establishes, which the ordinary legislature of the parliamentary legislative state cannot do."[99] Schmitt calls this synthesis of legislative and executive authority a "legal" virtue of the decision itself.[100] As he wrote in the *Verfassungslehre*, "The practice of the Napoleonic plebiscite was based on the democratic principle of the constituent power of the people; Constitutional breaches/violations could thus easily be rectified through the approval/compliance of the People."[101]

Schmitt's preference for presidential authority might seem predictable enough, but the source of its popular legitimacy bears closer inspection. One might, for example, point to the democratic legitimacy conferred by direct national election. In parliamentary elections, the demos made a momentary appearance, certainly. However, while the people were thereby present, they were not linked directly to their representatives. Joseph Bendersky affirms Schmitt's critique in this respect, noting that parliamentary elections in which voters could only choose among lists established in secret by leaders of the parties, rather than individual candidates—"constituted 'a roll-call of the standing-party army' and, in effect, a plebiscite."[102] However, Schmitt goes even further, not only reducing parliamentary representation to a plebiscite, but also degrading it below that of the president.

> The people can only respond yes or no. They cannot advise, deliberate, or discuss. They cannot govern or administer. . . . Above all, they also cannot pose a question, but can only answer with yes or no. . . . If the people are presented a series of party lists instead of an answerable question, lists that, once again, are produced in the deeply obscure shadows of party committee rooms; and if the government avoids posing a decisive question through parliamentary dissolutions; then the "election" process itself becomes pointless. In terms of its significance, the process is no longer an election but a plebiscite. However, because of the lack of an answerable question, or in the best case only through

a fortunate accident, it does not even become an actual plebiscite expressing a yes or no.[103]

The parliamentary legislative state, once it is understood to express the momentary presence of a democratic will, simply becomes an unwieldy and hypocritical—and most importantly, unpopular—form of popular dictatorship.

In the transition Schmitt describes from statutory to plebiscitary legitimacy, we find a shift not only in the object but the nature of democratic "confidence." In abnormal times, confidence has less to do with predictable norms than with an ill-defined competence. Whereas it once supported stable habits of obedience to predictable norms, it now accrued to an agent empowered to impose form on a divided, unstable society. At some threshold of social conflict and situational instability, confidence in statutory law, with its general and stable character, becomes "inappropriate," as it no longer corresponds to a situation of similar duration. Parliamentary legislation, under abnormal conditions was at once too volatile to produce durable law and too slow for effective responses to emergent crises. The executive was simply more capable of responding to rapidly shifting situations. In support of this executive, Schmitt places faith in law on a continuum with faith in will. By reiterating "confidence" in both cases, he effectively conflates trust in the "reason and justice" of parliamentary legislation with faith in the personal will of the president. By preserving the form "represented" by the classical legislative state, namely democratic will in the form of public confidence, he treats presidential plebiscites as "substantive" law. Thus, he describes plebiscitary rule as a "recognition of the substantive characteristics and capacities of the German people."[104] The plebiscitary president thus appears a kind of commissarial dictator, an agent of the concrete national will of the people unaccountable to their legal representatives.

Democratic Romanticism

Although Schmitt's arguments in *Legality and Legitimacy* internally cohere, more or less, they hardly explain popular confidence, particularly that of the outvoted minority, in presidential competence. Indeed, the personal legitimacy of the president seems hardly more plausible than the formal legitimacy Schmitt denied parliamentary statutes. Regarding the latter, he writes:

An unconditional equivalence of law with the results of any particular formal process . . . would only be blind subordination to the pure decision of the offices entrusted with lawmaking, in other words, a decision detached from every substantive relation to law and justice. . . . It would be *sic volo sic jubeo* in its most naïve form and only conceivable psychologically on the basis of the remnant of some superstition or as residues of an earlier, substantively richer religious-like belief.[105]

One might argue the democratic support for presidential rule rested on just such a naïve religious-like belief, if it exists at all. After all, the majority who elects the president is, like the parliamentary majority Schmitt describes, "heterogeneous."[106] McCormick describes Schmitt's preference for executive power as "spiritual." While this is no doubt the case, it remains to be considered how this spiritual preference (or the "myth" of the presidential mandate) is cultivated in the public themselves. As Schmitt had argued earlier, "spiritual" belief was itself sustained by symbolic concentration.[107] As he had in *Roman Catholicism and Political Form*, Schmitt links the supralegal authority of the early modern governmental state to its possession of various symbols or "emblems." In this case, however, the latter command not an ethos but a pathos.

> The governmental state does not have so much an ethos as a great pathos. Its principle became most visible . . . in the catalogue of representative emblems of the princes, who clothed their personal realm with words like *majestas*, *splendor*, *excellentia*, *eminenta*, *honor*, and *glory*. It is the great pathos of *glory* and *honor* that the Prussian administrative state of Friedrich Wilhelm I and Frederick the Great could not deny itself. Already in the seventeenth century, the republican-democratic *vertu* opposed the governmental state's principle as a polemical counterconcept against honor, seeking to disqualify the representative quality of honor and to expose representation itself as mere "theater," while republican-democratic *vertu* set the homogeneous people's democratic and self-identical presence against the representation of the court.[108]

Thus, Schmitt once again contrasts traditional authority with republican-democratic virtue. However, neither was appropriate in a highly modern, volatile society. Having no faith in democratic virtue or the capacity for collective self-organization—and lacking the grounds for a traditional "ethos" of belief—he instead imagined a demos unified by "confidence," a rather pale echo of that pathos once inspired by eminence, glory, and honor. Unlike glory and honor, with their ties to longstanding economic and cultural hierarchies, this confidence was drawn from the volatile, technologically mediated public sphere of an advanced capitalist mass democracy. It was formed not by ritual mediations, but by the capture of transient energies in unstable constellations of symbols detached from traditional spaces and modes of civic life.[109]

However principled Schmitt's own confidence in the executive might have been, the same threat to form and stability he attributed to the unrestrained legislative state would soon be manifest in its authoritarian counterpart. Schmitt's conflation of law and executive measures, placing legal and personal authority on a continuum of "representation," has unavoidably been read in the light of his subsequent justification of Hitler's executive excesses, which were justified in very similar terms to those Schmitt developed in 1932. Schmitt's merging of personal and legal power in the figure of the president, certainly, was complicit with Fascist modes of self-representation,[110] including Hitler's patently absurd pretense to constitutionalism.

In this light, Schmitt's justification of presidential autonomy has been read as a dissimulating, opportunistic, or "occasional" rationalization. As John McCormick notes, Schmitt's description of Napoleon as an instance of a "precarious" plebiscitary executive with limited "independence" is implausible at best.[111] While there might be limits to charismatic authority, they hardly make actions taken within them substantively democratic. As Weber argued, the success of the charismatic leader can live just as well on fatalism, despair, and cynicism as it can on faith or trust. He writes, "it has to be clearly realized that the plebiscitarian leadership of parties entails the 'soullessness' of the following, their intellectual proleterianization, one might say. In order to be a useful apparatus, a machine in the American sense . . . the following of such a leader must obey him blindly."[112] In Schmitt's treatment of the plebiscite, similarly, McCormick finds democratic will effectively giving way to passive assent. "Like Odysseus's sailors or Caligari's zombie, the demos have no real will apart from its master's direction or manipulation."[113] Taking an example from Schmitt's earlier writings, we might instead compare the subjective orientation Schmitt ascribes to the *demos* in *Legality and Legitimacy* to that he earlier identified with the Romantic. Indeed, Schmitt's formulation of the "ethical" orientation of the Romantic can readily be mapped onto his later depiction of the acclamatory masses. "His freedom consists in 'assent,' in a feeling of value, a judgment, and a criticism. It is precisely the ethics of rationalistic systems that favor limiting the person to 'assenting' to the immutable nomological necessity of the event. In romanticism, however, this idea also is sentimentalized and deformed in an emotive direction."[114] Similarly, the public in *Legality and Legitimacy* assents not to anything rationally necessary, but rather to the charismatic authority of the executive. Its confidence exhibits the flexibility of romantic abstractions, "whose empty formulas can be adapted to any state of affairs."[115] In this text, however, Schmitt asserts, "affirmation and denials . . . should not be regarded as expressions of resolute activity."[116] He had only derision for the romantic personalities that so closely resemble the democratic masses the legitimacy of whose will he later asserted. Like Schlegel or Müller, these masses were capable of assimilating all manner of fusions of opposites, subject to every "powerful suggestion . . . without [their] own center of gravity."[117]

Elsewhere, Schmitt notes the prevalent condescension toward the masses on the part of both politicians and political scientists. "In the treatment of the masses, posterlike, insistent suggestion or—as Walter Lippman says in his very shrewd, although too psychological, American book *Public Opinion*—the 'symbol' appears."[118] However, if the public is romantic, it is not simply inert material to be shaped by the leader. In this respect, McCormick's analogies appear somewhat misleading. A zombie, after all, can neither refuse nor really affirm its master's instructions. It is not an enthusiast. The romantic, by contrast, is a fund of intensity that poeticizes both the status quo and its rupture. The masses, likewise, are imbued with confidence that infuses the measures of the leader with an amorphous legitimacy regardless of their practical content.[119] Their participation is thus "substantial," yet not instructive. The "subjective freedom" demanded by bourgeois society is thereby maintained without posing any threat to objective order. Theirs is a conservative poetics, allowing the "state" to exist across any number of institutional changes in form, however revolutionary.[120] Following Schmitt's description of romanticism's purely "aesthetic productivity" we might call this *theatrical democracy*, referring not only to the leader's aesthetic production but also to the receptive attitude of those who follow. It is this aestheticization, that is, the interpellation of the masses as a stimulated, powerfully receptive audience of political spectacle, that Walter Benjamin argues must be countered with a politicization of art, one that engages a critical responsiveness.[121] Indeed, Schmitt might be said to ironically prefigure Benjamin's formulations when he declares that the notion of the "state as a work of art" is the "core of all political romanticism."[122]

It is well known that Fascist ideology was characterized by a promiscuous "combination of opposites," blending class, religious, technological, and economic symbols.[123] The Fascist self-conception as a passage from Idea to material form thus involved significant dissimulation of the iterative dimension of its ideology. As we have seen, Schmitt's earlier account of "persuasive speech" as a discursive production of a *complexio oppositorum* pointed to this possibility. In the case of Fascism, new forms of representation, image-based media in particular, enhanced the manufacture of what Benjamin called a false "aura."[124] Rather than the Church and the pope, it was the Party and Hitler who personified a combination of economic, aesthetic, and cultural values, a personification sustained by a proliferation of images and slogans.[125] Recalling our earlier discussion, we might say that with the ascension of Hitler the antichrist had indeed become pope. However, the ethical community that comprised the "visible church" had been replaced by specular masses. The practice of Fascism was thus at odds with Schmitt's attempts to distinguish sovereign authority from the murky sources of romantic myths, and realized all his fears concerning the latter's volatility. Under fascism, the authoritarian mobilization of collective will by way of an identification of enemies became a mytho-poetical production whose main object was the generation of surplus identity and authority, leading to a genocidal, and ultimately suicidal, intensification of conflict.[126]

It is not my intention here to analyze in detail the aesthetic dimensions of Schmitt's political discourse, much less their relationship to the aesthetic politics of the Nazi period. However, we might see in Schmitt's analysis of the romantic politician a prefiguring of the direction in which executive autonomy would soon lead, namely an occasional approach to enemies. Like the romantic, Schmitt rejected both mechanical and normative constraints on the agency of the sovereign. Thornhill is thus right to describe Schmitt's decisionism as another form of occasionalism.[127] Of course, the use of enemies as occasions symbolically and rhetorically enhanced incitements to indiscriminate struggles is what Schmitt tried, and failed, to forestall in Germany by establishing an independent source of their designation. Yet he could not maintain the distinction between divine and subjective occasionalism. The theatrical executive he supported was not Hobbes's sovereign but the politician Weber described in his own analysis of plebiscitary mass democracy, an "actor" who aims at an "impression."[128] In the Fascist movement, like the romantic psyche, "a complex of powerful political energies is not able to find its objective, and it strikes an occasional point with great force."[129] Schmitt illustrated this "problem of ontology" by way of Don Quixote, whose idea of Dulcinea became an occasional motive rather than a guiding objective. "What matters is only that, for him, she remains the object of the ideal devotion that inspires him to great deeds."[130] Likewise, as the site on which a great combination of enmity was displaced, the Jew became the site of an excessive hostility transcending concrete social and economic struggles.

It has been my contention that one can find in Schmitt's writings not only a potentially Fascist aesthetic, but also insights regarding its operation. Insofar as this is the case, they highlight potential directions for a critical response along the lines Walter Benjamin recommended, much as one can synthesize an antidote from venom. In *Roman Catholicism and Political Form*, Schmitt describes the aesthetic techniques that sustained the authority of the Church, including sculpture, painting, and rhetoric. In *Political Romanticism*, he highlights the discursive techniques (superlatives, generalities, ternary paraphrase) that give Adam Müller's writing its own "suggestive force."[131] In his subsequent defense of sovereign authority, however, he moved away from discursive analysis in favor his own abstractions and embellishments. For Adam Müller, political situations were occasions for a poetic activity that could romanticize any predominant situation. For Schmitt rhetorical techniques served to unite diverse values in support of a distinct political aim. Taking in properly coded terms Leo Strauss's assertion that Schmitt's commitment to the political was ultimately "moral," we might see in Schmitt's political aesthetics—as in his strategic positioning—the dangers of an elitism that knowingly promotes romantic passivity for the masses, even as it succumbs to its own fantasies of a cool juridical gaze on the part of the ruler.[132] By contrast, we might follow Benjamin's call for a politicization of democratic aesthetics, even, or especially, when it calls into question the legitimacy of rule itself.

Notes

1. See Carl Schmitt, *Roman Catholicism and Political Form*, trans. G. L. Ulmen (Westport, CT: Greenwood Press, 1996), 25–26, hereafter *RCPF*.
2. Schmitt, *RCPF*, 26.
3. Schmitt, *RCPF*, 27.
4. Schmitt, *RCPF*, 17–18. Indeed, Schmitt notes, the objective "owner" of capital was disappearing rapidly in the "joint-stock companies and other juridical persons." Compare Carl Schmitt, *The Crisis of Parliamentary Democracy*, trans. Ellen Kennedy (Cambridge, MA: MIT Press, 1988), 48, hereafter *CPD*, on the "sinister and crazy" suggestion that war be fought for economic security.
5. Schmitt, *RCPF*, 19.
6. Schmitt, *RCPF*, 20.
7. I examine Sorel's argument along these lines in "The Myth of the Multitude," *The Empire's New Clothes* (New York: Routledge, 2003).
8. Schmitt, *CPD*, 61.
9. Schmitt, *CPD*, 59.
10. See Karl Marx, "Contribution to the Critique of Hegel's Philosophy of Right: Introduction," in *The Marx-Engels Reader*, ed. Robert C. Tucker (New York: Norton, 1978), 62 (italics in original).
11. Schmitt, *CPD*, 74.

12. Schmitt, *CPD*, 73–74. I depart slightly from Kennedy's translation of this passage, which gives *häufen* as "intensifying" rather than accumulating. Cf. Schmitt, *Die geistesgeschichtliche Lage des heutigen Parlamentarismus* (München: Duncker & Humblot, 1926), 87.

13. V. I. Lenin, *What Is to Be Done* (New York: International Publishers, 1969), 76–77.

14. See Ellen Kennedy, *Constitutional Failure, Carl Schmitt in Weimar* (Durham, NC: Duke University Press, 2004), 112.

15. Schmitt, *CPD*, 75. Schmitt's descriptive pronouncements on *terrisme* are often confused for prescriptions, which is not to say that he did not prefer nation to class.

16. Simona Draghici, a translator of Schmitt's work, implies as much. A myth, she writes, "incorporates oppositions, structural as well as ideational, reconciling them, and so rendering tolerable experiences that otherwise are incoherent." Draghici, "Introduction," in Carl Schmitt, *Land and Sea* (Corvallis, OR: Plutarch Press, 1997), viii.

17. Carl Schmitt, *Römischer Katholizismus und politische Form* (Stuttgart: Klett-Cotta, 1984), 5, hereafter *RK*. My translation.

18. See Benedict Anderson, *Imagined Communities* (New York: Verso, 1991). In subsequent chapters, I discuss Schmitt's response to the dissolution of the territorial forms on which the nation-state arose when these forces are disaggregated and spread across the globe by way of international media, Diaspora, and global markets.

19. Cf. Gopal Balakrishnan, *The Enemy* (New York: Verso, 2000), 62.

20. Chris Thornhill reads Schmitt's grounding of executive authority in the friend-enemy antithesis as a "mode of consciously secular politics." Cf. Chris Thornhill, *Political Theory in Modern Germany* (Cambridge, UK: Polity Press, 1999), 77.

21. Cf. Schmitt, *CP*, 33. "The friend, enemy, and combat concepts receive their real meaning precisely because they refer to the real possibility of physical killing. War follows from enmity."

22. Schmitt, *CP*, 38; Schmitt, *Der Begriff des Politischen* (Berlin: Duncker & Humblot, 2002), 39. See also Schmitt, *CP*, 26: The friend-enemy distinction denotes "the utmost intensity of a union or separation."

23. Schmitt, *CP*, 62.

24. As Deleuze and Guattari argue, Fascism "resonated" with otherwise fragmented local affiliations and conflicts. Cf. Gilles Deleuze and Felix Guattari, *A Thousand Plateaus* (Minneapolis: University of Minnesota Press, 1987), 214.

25. Deleuze and Guattari, *A Thousand Plateaus*, 27. My emphasis.

26. Deleuze and Guattari, *A Thousand Plateaus*, 29.

27. William Scheuerman relates Hans Morgenthau's claim to have influenced Schmitt's arguments on this point. He writes, "In fact, Schmitt's 1932 study tends to drop misleading imagery of politics as a distinct or separate sphere, instead following Morgenthau's conceptualization of politics as concerning conflicts characterized by intense enmity." Scheuerman, "Carl Schmitt and Hans Morgenthau: Realism and Beyond," in *Reconsidering Realism: The Legacy of Hans J. Morgenthau*, ed. Michael

Williams (Oxford: Oxford University Press, in press, 2007). However, we can see that even if responding to such a thesis, Schmitt adopts a more complex view, whereby quantity transforms into quality, preserving both the role of a plurality of antagonisms in generating a political opposition and the clarity of the distinction between such an opposition and other antagonisms.

28. Schmitt, CP, 28.

29. Schmitt, CP, 29, fn. 9.

30. Cf. Carl Von Clausewitz, On War, trans. Michael Howard and Peter Paret (Princeton, NJ: Princeton University Press, 1984), 137–38.

31. Schmitt, CP, 34.

32. Schmitt, CP, 35.

33. Schmitt, CP, 27; Schmitt, Der Begriff des Politischen, 27.

34. By definition, for Schmitt, nonpolitical (private) sources of decision regarding life and death (e.g., that of the head of a family concerning the vendetta) must be suspended in the case of war. Cf. Schmitt, CP, 47.

35. Cf. Schmitt, CP, 39: "Should the counterforces be strong enough to hinder a war desired by the state that was contrary to their interests or principles but not sufficiently capable themselves of deciding about war, then a unified political entity would no longer exist."

36. Schmitt, CP, 43–44; Schmitt, Der Begriff des Politischen, 43.

37. Cf. Schmitt, CP, 38–39.

38. Cf. Schmitt, CP, 29: "The political is the most intense and extreme antagonism, and every concrete antagonism becomes that much more political the closer it approaches the most extreme point, that of the friend-enemy grouping." See also 58: "The weight of the political is determined by the intensity of alignments according to which the decisive associations and dissociations adjust themselves."

39. Schmitt, CP, 39. See also 29–30: "In its entirety the state as an organized political entity decides for itself the friend-enemy distinction."

40. William Connolly, Pluralism (Durham, NC: Duke University Press, 2005), 145.

41. Cf. Benjamin, "The Work of Art in the Age of Its Mechanical Reproducibility," in Jennings, ed. Walter Benjamin: Selected Writings, vol. 4 (Cambridge, MA: Harvard University Press, 2003).

42. Schmitt, CP, 30.

43. Schmitt, CP, 31, fn. 12.

44. Should party politics attain the status of political antagonism, internal antagonisms would overwhelm the unity of the state, a situation Schmitt describes as civil war. Schmitt, CP, 32.

45. Kennedy, Constitutional Failure, 108. Bendersky chides Schmitt for effectively criticizing Versailles in academic mode, without thinking of the resulting "demoralizing effects . . . on German society." Joseph Bendersky, Carl Schmitt, Theorist for the Reich (Princeton, NJ: Princeton University Press, 1983), 54.

46. See Karl Polanyi, *The Great Transformation* (Boston: Beacon Press, 2001), chapter 20.

47. See Balakrishnan, who argues that Schmitt "surreptitiously reintroduced the state as the natural subject of political life." Balakrishnan, *The Enemy*, 110.

48. Cf. Schmitt, CP, 30: "Finally even more banal forms of politics appear, forms which assume parasite- and caricature-like configurations. What remains here from the original friend-enemy grouping is only some sort of antagonistic moment, which manifests itself in all sorts of tactics and practices, competitions and intrigues; and the most peculiar dealings and manipulations are called politics."

49. Schmitt's theory of the constitution thus "undermines the legitimacy of parliament." Cf. Balakrishnan, *The Enemy*, 95; Bendersky, *Carl Schmitt*, 97–100; Kennedy, *Constitutional Failure*, 134.

50. Carl Schmitt, *Verfassungslehre* (Berlin: Duncker & Humblot, 1989), 88. My translation. Other articles referred to the German people "giving" themselves a constitution. Cf. Schmitt, *Verfassungslehre*, 23–24.

51. See Bendersky, *Carl Schmitt*, chapter 6.

52. Duncan Kelly, "Carl Schmitt's Theory of Representation," *Journal of the History of Ideas* 65.1, 2004.

53. Quoted in Kelly, "Carl Schmitt's Theory of Representation," 118.

54. Schmitt, *Verfassungslehre*, 77–79. My translation. Italics in original.

55. Schmitt, *Verfassungslehre*, 23.

56. Schmitt, *Verfassungslehre*, 228. My translation.

57. Schmitt, *Verfassungslehre*, 231 Quoted in Kennedy, *Constitutional Failure*, 129. Compare Schmitt's description of the various sources of democratic "equality" in *The Crisis of Parliamentary Democracy*, which can be based on civic virtue, religious convictions, or membership in a particular nation. Schmitt, CPD, 9–10.

58. Kennedy, *Constitutional Failure*, 95.

59. Kelly, "Carl Schmitt's Theory of Representation," 122.

60. Kelly, "Carl Schmitt's Theory of Representation, 124–25.

61. Kelly, "Carl Schmitt's Theory of Representation, 117–18.

62. Kelly, "Carl Schmitt's Theory of Representation, 131.

63. Kelly, "Carl Schmitt's Theory of Representation, 132.

64. Kelly, "Carl Schmitt's Theory of Representation," 120.

65. Schmitt, *Verfassungslehre*, 83–84. My translation. One might just as well describe voting as another kind of acclamation, one that can easily take a simple yes/no form in votes of "confidence." Weber treats applause and voting as analogous ways most people participate in politics. "We are all 'occasional' politicians when we cast our ballot or consummate a similar expression of intention, such as applauding." Max Weber, "Politics as a Vocation," in *From Max Weber*, ed. H. H. Gerth and C. Wright Mills. (New York: Oxford University Press, 1946), 83. See also Schmitt, *Verfassungslehre*, 243–44 on the public character of constituent power and its acclamatory form.

66. Schmitt, *Verfassungslehre*, 85.

67. On the mix of direct and representative action, see Kelly, "Carl Schmitt's Theory of Representation," 119–20. As Ellen Kennedy also notes, Schmitt's depiction of the formation of the German Republic in 1918 out of a combination of representative and direct action conflicted with that of the Supreme Court, which emphasized "the continuity of state institutions." Cf. Kennedy, *Constitutional Failure*, 97.

68. Schmitt, *CPD*, 16.

69. Carl Schmitt, *Legality and Legitimacy*, trans and ed. Jeffrey Seitzer (Durham, NC: Duke University Press, 2004), hereafter, *LL*.

70. Ellen Kennedy describes this article, rather than Article 48, as Schmitt's primary concern. Cf. Kennedy, *Constitutional Failure*, 7.

71. Schmitt, *LL*, 30.

72. Schmitt, *LL*, 35.

73. Schmitt, *Verfassungslehre*, 31, quoted in Kennedy, *Constitutional Failure*, 96.

74. Cf. Schmitt, *LL*, 19 and 24–25 on "legislative reservation."

75. Schmitt, *LL*, 24. See also 41–42.

76. Carl Schmitt. *Legaliät und Legitimität* (Munchen: Duncker & Humblot, 1932), 28.

77. Schmitt, *LL*, 20–21, 28.

78. Schmitt, *LL*, 31–32.

79. See Schmitt, *LL*, 9.

80. Schmitt, "Further Development of the Total State in Germany," (1933) in Carl Schmitt, *Four Articles*, trans. Simona Draghici (Corvallis, OR: Plutarch Press, 1999).

81. Schmitt, *LL*, 44.

82. Schmitt, *LL*, 29. See also 36: "equal chance loses its persuasiveness."

83. Schmitt, "Further Development of the Total State," 23.

84. Schmitt, *LL*, 33.

85. Schmitt, *LL*, 46–48, 56–57.

86. Schmitt, *LL*, 42, 53, respectively.

87. Schmitt, *LL*, 41.

88. Schmitt, *LL*, 52–53.

89. Schmitt, *LL*, 52.

90. Schmitt, *LL*, 54.

91. Cf. Schmitt, *LL*, 55–56.

92. Schmitt, *LL*, 90.

93. Schmitt, *LL*, 12–13.

94. Cf. Bendersky, *Carl Schmitt*, 110–11.

95. Schmitt, *LL*, 83. Jurgen Habermas later makes the same observation in *The Structural Transformation of the Public Sphere* (Cambridge, MA: MIT Press, 1991), 179.

96. See Schmitt, *LL*, 81.

97. Schmitt, *LL*, 83.

98. Schmitt, *LL*, 32, 34.

99. Schmitt, *LL*, 71. See also Schmitt, *LL*: "The extraordinary lawmaker can create accomplished facts."

100. Schmitt, *LL*, 9.

101. Schmitt, *Verfassunglehre*, 92. My translation.

102. Bendersky, *Carl Schmitt*, 110.

103. Schmitt, *LL*, 89–90.

104. Schmitt, *LL*, 93.

105. Schmitt, *LL*, 21.

106. Cf. Robert Dahl, "The Myth of the Presidential Mandate," *Political Science Quarterly* 105 (Autumn 1990): 355–72.

107. Cf. Schmitt, *RCPF*, 20.

108. Schmitt, *LL*, 8.

109. See Walter Benjamin, "The Work of Art in the Age of Its Mechanical Reproducibility." For a more recent discussion of presidential media tactics, see Douglas Kellner, "Presidential Politics: The Movie," *American Behavioral Scientist*, 46.4 (2002): 467–86.

110. This operated at a variety of levels. On Hitler and the Nazi preoccupation with the semblance of legal continuity amidst their destruction of constitutional restrictions, see George Schwab, *The Challenge of the Exception* (Berlin: Duncker & Humblot, 1970), 118.

111. See McCormick, "Introduction" to Schmitt, *LL*, xli.

112. Weber, "Politics as a Vocation," 113. On the plebiscite as a dissimulation of executive autonomy, see William Scheuerman, *Liberal Democracy and the Social Acceleration of Time* (Baltimore, MD: Johns Hopkins University Press, 2004), 93–94.

113. McCormick, "Introduction," xl.

114. Carl Schmitt, *Political Romanticism*, trans. Guy Oakes (Cambridge, MA: MIT Press, 1986), 94, hereafter, *PR*.

115. Schmitt, *PR*, 103.

116. Schmitt, *PR*, 100.

117. Cf. Schmitt, *PR*, 128.

118. Schmitt, *CPD*, 6. Regarding Schmitt's jab at Lippman's "psychological" approach, recall Schmitt's account of the reciprocal determination of psyche, symbol, and material ritual in his discussion of the *complexio oppositorum*.

119. Brian Massumi interprets Reagan's popularity along these lines. Cf. Massumi, "The Autonomy of Affect," in *Parables for the Virtual* (Durham, NC: Duke University Press, 2002).

120. Schmitt, *PR*, 127. See also Schmitt, *PR*, 126, on the poeticization of obedience, e.g., paying taxes as "giving presents to the beloved."

121. I discuss Benjamin in previous work. Cf. Kam Shapiro, *Sovereign Nations, Carnal States* (Ithaca, NY: Cornell University Press, 2003), chapter 4.

122. Schmitt, *PR*, 125.

123. Cf. George Mosse, *Masses and Man* (New York: Howard Fertig, 1980), 230; Jeffrey Schnapp, *Staging Fascism* (Stanford, CA: Stanford University Press, 1996), 6; Andrew Hewitt, *Fascist Modernism* (Stanford, CA: Stanford University Press, 1993), 46.

124. Cf. Walter Benjamin, "The Work of Art," 158.

125. Cf. Eric Michaud, *Un Art De L'Éternité* (Paris: Gallimard, 1996).

126. Hannah Arendt thus describes totalitarian politics as characterized by a struggle to "prevent normalization." See Arendt, *The Origins of Totalitarianism* (San Diego, CA: Harcourt, 1976), 391. Schwab compares the image of the Jew under Nazism to that of Sorel's bourgeois class, the object of mythological hatred. Cf. Schwab, *Challenge*, 133.

127. Cf. Thornhill, *Political Theory*, 79.

128. Weber, "Politics as a Vocation," 116.

129. Schmitt, *PR*, 147. Here he describes the murder of a relatively insignificant figure on the basis of an active political will that is nonetheless romantic, and that blends discrete political hostilities with something like aesthetic hatred ("baseness and vileness").

130. Schmitt, *PR*, 148.

131. Schmitt, *PR*, 138.

132. John McCormick takes up this critique of Straussian positions in his introduction to Schmitt, *LL*, xlii.

CHAPTER FOUR

~

Globalization and Nihilism

Following his collaboration with the Hitler regime between 1933 and 1936, cut short by understandable suspicions of his loyalty on the part of the SS, Schmitt witnessed its catastrophic rise and fall from the sidelines.[1] After the war, he spent a year and a half in American internment camps and underwent a brief trial at Nuremberg before his release into relative obscurity.[2] In works composed during and after these events, he sought grounds for juridical order other than the personal authority of an executive or the homogeneity of a national will, turning his attention to the international order within which both are situated. While he recognized the attenuation of national sovereignty, Schmitt still dismissed the sublimation of politics by positive law and liberal capitalism. If anything, the image of a "self-organizing" society was even more absurd when applied to a welter of international flows of capital, media, weapons, and ideas. A stable juridical order still depended upon a substantial, or "concrete," order whose boundaries could only be secured by extra-legal means. The question was, where and how, or by whom, could a normal situation be identified or created? The distinction between norm and exception had begun to circulate beyond discrete borders and institutions. International laws were even more easily instrumentalized or circumvented than those of the Weimar parliaments he had criticized earlier. Rejecting what he saw as the false pretenses and real dangers of global sovereignty (associated with the League of Nations and the United States, respectively), Schmitt proposed the alternative of a new pluralism of large federal territories or "*Grossräume*," a term developed during the expansion of the Third Reich.[3] He declared all attempts to realize global norms utopian and "nihilistic."[4]

Schmitt's exposition of the spatial foundation of law, and thus of the nihilistic or "utopian" implications of global politics, will be the focus of this chapter. It involves a complex theory of political territory, situating his notion of the exception in spatial categories deriving from the history of international law, and links his critique of positive law to the notion of a "concrete order." Schmitt's reconstruction of territoriality begins with *Land and Sea* (1942), a mythical narrative in which the distinction of norm and exception is inaugurated by the primordial separation of a terrestrial order from the chaos of the sea.[5] In *The Nomos of the Earth* (1950), he shifts from mythology to etymology, recovering the unity of law and territory signified by the Greek term, *nomos*. He argues that the secular international law of the modern European state system (*Jus Publicum Europaeum*) rested on an encompassing *nomos* comprising a combination of "order and localization," a distinctly European space characterized by shared cultural, economic, and technological features. Within this common space, warfare was constrained by reciprocal conventions regarding weapons, tactics, treatments of prisoners and civilians, and so forth. In Schmitt's new terms, European antagonists had been "just enemies." This hard-won modern notion was destroyed along with the erosion of the spatial order of the *Jus Publicum Europaeum* by a combination of legal, economic, technological, and political developments culminating in the First World War. Subsequent attempts on the part of the victors to criminalize war as such forgot the notion of just enemies and regressed to (secularized) medieval concepts of "just war." In just wars, the symmetry of antagonists and limits on the instruments of violence gave way to "discriminatory" conflicts that criminalized enemies and deprived them of both formal reciprocity and humanistic recognition. New military technologies, especially air power, not only enhanced the destructiveness of conflict but also compounded spatial and ethical confusions concerning friend and enemy, norm and exception. In Schmitt's late essay, *Theory of the Partisan* (1963), these threats concentrate in the figure of the partisan engaged in guerilla warfare, with its logic of terror and counterterror.[6]

In the face of these developments, Schmitt again struck the pose of the *Katechon*, seeking bulwarks against the dissolution of territorial distinctions and the chaotic proliferation of hostility.[7] In some respects, Schmitt's later work returns to the terms of his earlier Catholic writings, placing emphasis on ideas and mediating institutions that subtend both law and authority. Yet it does so in the context of a secular, pluralistic international order, substituting a decentered model of constituent power for the sovereign state, and an elastic civilization for national culture. Theological metaphors give way to new elemental myths, and technology conspires with human nature as a motor of destruction. These shifts in perspective and argument are reflected in new tropes that indicate the volatility of the global confluence of forces. They speak of a chastened, but not fatalistic struggle for an orderly *status quo* on the part of one who understands that every worldly normalcy comprises a tense equilibrium, a *modus vivendi* of contending forces. Finally, I argue they situate political theory among the forces that compromise the autonomy of politics Schmitt struggled to maintain.

Grounding a Legal Order

In *The Nomos of the Earth*, Schmitt describes the attenuation of political space as such. The dissolution of the territorial state system that had subtended the *Jus Publicum Europaeum*, culminating in the first World War, had undermined not only the European nation-state but the classical dichotomy between land and sea, and thus of the classical unity of "order and localization" (*Ordnung und Ortung*) on which all law was based. Schmitt elaborates the territorial basis of law through an etymology of the Greek term "*Nomos*." While it had come to be translated alternately as "law," signifying abstract codes, or "ruler," in the sense of arbitrary power, *Nomos* had originally denoted concrete forms of land-appropriation (*Landnahme*, literally "land taking").

> Not to lose the decisive connection between order and orientation, one should not translate *nomos* as law (in German, *Gesetz*), regulation, norm or any similar expression. *Nomos* comes from *nemein*—a [Greek] word that means both "to divide" and "to pasture." Thus *nomos* is the immediate form in which the political and social order of a people becomes spatially visible—the initial measure and division of pasture-land, i.e., the land-appropriation as well as the concrete order contained in it and following from it. In Kant's words, it is the "distributive law of mine and thine," or, to use an English term that expresses it so well, it is the "radical title."[8]

As the term "radical title" (as in *radicalis*, or root) indicates, all legal systems stem from a territorial order. Other precedents could be cited, such as Machiavelli's city founder, who "judged by two things: firstly, by his choice of a site for the construction of the new city; secondly, by the laws he draws up for it."[9] As Schmitt argued in *Political Theology*, "all law is situational," or as he puts it here, "law and order are one."[10] Furthermore, just as the situation was itself a function of a sovereign decision that distinguished the normal from the exception, the concrete order subtending law could be traced to a constituent act, in this case a founding territorial appropriation. Political space is not based on a *de facto status quo*, but a "constitutive act of spatial ordering" that establishes, concretely, the ground for religious and political order.[11] Displaying his usual orientation to archetypes, Schmitt describes subsequent evolutions of the term to denote formal statutes as "mere degenerations, evasions and disintegrations" of this original sense.[12] *Nomos* properly understood denotes neither positive law nor the inertia of tradition and custom. Rather, "nomos is precisely the full immediacy of a legal power not mediated by law; it is a constitutive historical event—an act of legitimacy [*Akt der Legitimität*], whereby the legality of a mere law first is made meaningful."[13] Schmitt thus links constituent power to a substantial order marked out from the earth as a whole, positing a form-giving "legal power" prior to formal legality. As Ulmen notes, Schmitt takes advantage of the connection in German of "Ur-teil" (a first division) and "Urteil" (a decision or judgment).[14] Ulmen's translation of *Ortung* as "orientation," which departs from the usual "location" or "positioning," also captures this dual sense of location and perspective.[15] In light of others' interpretation of the Greek term, however, it is clear that Schmitt's emphasis on a decisive act, or "taking," is tendentious, and ultimately misleading, a point to which we shall return below.

Like every political order, the European *nomos* was defined by its exception. The exception, understood spatially, follows from enclosure; beyond the bracketing of order lies an immeasurable difference and hostility, a dichotomy classically represented in the contrast between firm land and the chaos of the sea. The result, however, is not the elimination of antagonism (or suffering) within the former, but its containment, or recalling Schmitt's earlier discussion of Catholicism, its mediation. "In particular, it was not the abolition of war, but rather its bracketing that has been the great, core problem of every legal order."[16] Schmitt outlines various instances of such bracketing, focusing especially on that of medieval conflicts between Christian entities, as distinguished from crusades against non-Christian populations.[17] Christian empire, he emphasizes, served as a *Katechon*, defined by "concrete tasks and missions," namely preserving peace among its constituents rather than substituting its own autarky for that of the communities it encompassed. As instances of the latter "Ceasarism," Schmitt draws a parallel of early Christianity and the French Revolution.[18] Recalling again the terms of *Roman Catholicism and Political Form*, one might say the Church consecrated mediating institutions. "Peace, in particular, was not a free-floating, normative, general concept, but, rather, one oriented concretely to the peace of the empire, the territorial ruler, of the church, of the city, of the castle, of the marketplace, of the local juridical assembly."[19] The dissolution of the medieval *nomos* began in the thirteenth century, and culminated in the "anarchy" of the Thirty Years' War. However, the collapse of basic distinctions between peoples and territories, i.e., nihilism, would wait until the nineteenth century. In the interim between anarchy and nihilism, a new European *nomos* had its day.

The emergence of the *Jus Publicum Europaeum* and the consolidation of national territories began with a revolutionary act of spatial appropriation, namely the "discovery" of the New World. Colonial expansion opened up a new space of exception in which European powers could externalize their conflicts. This externalization was formalized in the Amity lines of the sixteenth and seventeenth centuries, which established the longitudinal boundary within which international law effectively bracketed intra-European conflict. "Beyond the line," in the open seas and the new land of the Americas, appropriation was unrestricted, and there could be no injustice, even among agents of European powers with common religious affiliations.[20] Among the theoretical reflections of this spatial innovation, Schmitt includes Hobbes's conception of a state of nature where "man is a wolf to man."[21] In this respect, the Amity line differed from the *Raya*, a boundary between the land appropriations of two different Christian powers. Rather than distinguishing between different political orders, it constituted a space outside legal territory altogether.[22] Even where Europeans chose to enter into treaties with non-Europeans, these had no status in international law, as the latter were considered leaderless nonowners. The fact that such freedom from justice resulted in genocidal violence against the inhabitants of these zones, and was predicated on a falsification of their own political constitutions, was a secondary concern.[23] "The crucial matter was the emergence of a secularized form of conflict among modern nation-states whereby the logic of *justa causa* (just cause) was replaced by the notion of a *justus hostis* (just enemy). Thus, the concept of colonies contained an ideological burden that affected, above all, European colonial powers."[24]

The notion of a just enemy might seem an abrupt departure from Schmitt's earlier formulations of antagonism. Arguably, it indicates Schmitt's desire to distance himself from the radical de-humanization of enemies on the part of the Nazis. However, it by no means indicates the sublimation of political distinctions by universal norms or the elevation of sovereign rule to a global scale. The *nomos* of the *Jus Publicum Europaeum* still distinguished Europe from its heathen other, but without the central source of adjudication proper to Catholic empire.[25] Instead, it was predicated on a "balance" composed of the mutually recognized sovereignty of states invested with the authority to decisively resolve civil conflicts within their borders. It distinguished justice not by the cause of conflict but the "type" of enemy. Drawing on Otto Brunner's *Land and Lordship* (1939), Schmitt traces the notion of a just enemy to the medieval feud, in which violence was limited by the reciprocal status of antagonists with shared notions of chivalry, rather than an independent state authority.[26] War was a "duel" bounded by conventional rules and expectations.[27] A similar distinction appeared earlier, recall, in Schmitt's discussion of *hostis* and *inimicus*, or public and private enemies in *The Concept of the Political*, where the aim was to distinguish properly political antagonism from class and party struggles.[28] As evidenced in the creedal wars of the late Middle Ages, however, the limitations posed to conflict by chivalry were hardly reliable. Just cause was a flexible concept that could be invoked in sectarian conflicts as well as crusades. It was Bodin who translated the epistemological skepticism of medieval authors regarding just cause into a properly modern, relativistic legal "decisionism."

> The asserted juridical right and moral legitimacy of one's own cause and the alleged injustice of the opponent's cause only sharpen and deepen the belligerents' hostility, surely in the most gruesome way. That we have learned from the feuds of the feudal age and from the creedal civil wars over theological truth and justice. But state sovereigns ended such murderous assertions of right and questions of guilt. That was the historical and intellectual accomplishment of the sovereign decision.[29]

Thus, Schmitt situates the decision, the heart of state sovereignty, within an encompassing order. Unlike the nihilism of global politics (the Hobbesian lawless "state of nature" beyond the line), the "anarchy" of the European state system was subtended by a common order exceeding "the precarious ties of sovereign wills 'autonomously joined together.'"[30]

In part III of *Nomos*, Schmitt unpacks the multiple sources of territorial symmetry involved in *Ordnung und Ortung*. Just as the state constitution rested on a "normal situation" and its identification by legitimate authorities, so the equal status of *justus hostis* of parties to a conflict on European soil was defined, on the one hand, by a "common opinion and a common recognition" and on the other by a "common constitutional standard."[31] Furthermore, European states shared economic systems, civil institutions, and military technologies.[32] The integrity of this order subtending European international law, in turn, was sustained not by a univocal sovereign, but "more or less elastic methods and procedures" that governed changes in territory, effectively limiting violence along a number of lines, including the neutrality of other states (guaranteed by the Great Powers), the protection of property, and the treatment of prisoners. Prisoners of war were not "objects of punishment and vengeance, or . . . hostages" and treaties could be concluded with amnesty clauses.[33] Crucially, the equality of warring parties was indicated and supported by the neutrality of third parties who remained agnostic regarding the *justa causa* of either party.[34]

The elasticity of the normal situation so described is striking, so extensive in fact that in Schmitt's new formulations, war *per se* no longer need be conceived as an exception. Waged between states that recognized each other's equivalent juridical status, European war was both public and "just."[35] Every other agent, however, was excluded from political recognition and became a "pirate, an outlaw." A war between equals was a "completely legal procedure" and gave rise to a new balance rather than mutual destruction.[36] Indeed, "Such wars are the opposite of disorder. They represent the highest form of order within the scope of human power. They are the only protection against a circle of increasing reprisals, i.e., against nihilistic hatreds and reactions whose meaningless goal lies in mutual destruction."[37] While territory changed hands in European conflicts, the basic structure of civil society remained intact. "The new sovereign was the lawgiver. It was taken for granted that he would . . . leave former laws and institutions essentially intact, and that he would respect vested interests and property rights."[38] On land, there was none of the "booty" of sea wars and piracy. Schmitt raises the notable exception of Revolutionary France, whose armies did not respect traditional property relations, but presumed to "free" conquered peoples.[39] Despite this interruption, however, the trend toward the integrity of the European territorial state resumed (following the restoration of a balanced order with the Congress of Vienna in 1814–1815). Ultimately, when combined with the democratic principle of self-determination in the nineteenth century, whereby a democratic "people" was equated with a national territory, it intensified to the point where, "The idea of the identity and continuity of the state was stronger than was any legitimacy or even legality."[40]

It might seem as though Schmitt resolves the tension between law and legitimacy by the Hegelian procedure he formerly repudiated, subsuming both power and form in a peristalsis not of spirit but of *nomos*.[41] Along these lines, Frederic Jameson argues, "for Schmitt the concept of *nomos* is a kind of equivalent of the function of the "mode of production" for Marxism; that is, it names a structure of totality that has taken various historical forms."[42] Instead, we could say of *nomos* what Marx said of the commodity. It appears simple at first, but abounds in metaphysical subtleties (and, like the commodity, arises from a series of complex material interactions). The phrase "concrete order" can be deceptive, since the foundation to which Schmitt refers is not a given set of institutions, or even a fixed territory (though passages can easily be found that imply one or both). "Every order of international law must guarantee . . . not the given territorial *status quo* . . . with all its many details . . . but rather its fundamental *nomos*—its spatial structure, the unity of order and orientation."[43] As Schmitt reminds his readers, "we must remember that a concrete order of international law mostly consists of uniting and blending [*Verbindung und Verschränkung*] several diverse orders."[44]

This "uniting and blending" of diverse orders recalls the constitution of Rousseau's Social Contract described in chapter 2, as well as the operations Schmitt attributed to both the Catholic *complexio oppositorum* and the Marxist "myth," each of which combined diverse sources of legitimacy that also became objects of strategic and rhetorical manipulation. More specifically, *nomos* can be seen as a more elaborate take on what Schmitt formerly called the *terrisme*—shaped by various cultural traditions and their mythological synthesis—that gave nationalism its political force. Like *terrisme*, *nomos* denotes neither an organic tradition, nor an objective spatial situation.[45] In *The Nomos of the Earth*, a bracketed spatial order, rather than a biological race or a psychological "spirit," is the basis of customs and habits that distinguish a people from humanity generally and give substance to their legal codes.[46] At the same time, while all territorial orders rest on constitutive acts, Schmitt considers certain markers of spatiality more durable or authentic than others (e.g., that of the northern hemisphere, and therefore of the "nordic race").[47] "Not every invasion or temporary occupation is a land-appropriation that founds an order . . . every seizure of land is not a *nomos*, although conversely, *nomos*, understood in our sense of the term, always includes a land-based order and orientation."[48] As Schmitt explains in *Land and Sea*, "A space revolution presupposes more than just setting foot on land previously unknown. It assumes the transformation of the notion of space at all levels."[49] Among these levels, Schmitt includes the placement of figures in space in Renaissance painting by way of perspective, and the emergence of acoustical space with new musical forms. Additionally, we should not forget the importance of the polemical distinction between this order and that "beyond the line." As Franz Neumann points out, the Nazis were able to make a case for their membership in an international legal order by placing Soviet Russia in the latter position.[50]

Despite Schmitt's references to "taking" and a "constitutive act" then, it would seem from his own account that the territorial balance of modern Europe—like the nation he described in the *Verfassungslehre*—was the work neither of a single sovereign nor a singular "act of legitimacy." A concrete order (like the "normal situation" described in *Political Theology*) does not arise simply from the marking of a boundary, but is the result of overlapping processes and activities that distinguish both spaces and modes of activity. Moreover, the revolutionary discovery of the New World itself had a plurality of sources, namely a historical merging of maritime technological innovations with a global spatial consciousness passed down from Rome's earlier cultural expansion. Seneca's idea of a spherical earth and "sentiment of a vaster space" was carried to Columbus, who found in them "the goading and the encouragement he needed to undertake his voyage."[51] One could say the creative act (e.g., "taking") that establishes a territorial order takes part in a Heideggerian "revealing," combining and synthesizing linguistic, geographical, cultural, and ethnic distinctions.[52] Schmitt's account of *nomos* thus involves a combination of process and enactment, becoming and deciding akin to that already identified in his earlier formulations of the political. George Schwab aptly describes Schmitt's concrete order as a "fusion" of norm and decision.[53]

Schmitt expressly refuses Bergson's opposition of an intellectualized space and an instinctual or "concrete" time.[54] Territory is itself characterized by action and becoming rather than abstract "intelligence" or a simple material "fact."[55] The *nomos* subtending the European order allowed for this dynamism, accommodating not only conflicts between states, but also the emergence of new political entities. Schmitt thus refers to the "possible or potential statehood" of insurgents, a potentiality he earlier attributed to political groupings that appear at a threshold of intensity in *The Concept of the Political*.[56] Here as well, the shift from potential to actual is facilitated by acts of recognition that transform the character of those entities they recognize. "Any recognition that a Great Power gives to another state's insurgents intensifies, in a very effective way, the moral, juridical, propagandistic, and military fighting potential of these insurgents, traitors, and saboteurs. In view of this fact, all claims to a purely factual and declarative character of recognition are untrue."[57] As an example, Schmitt mentions the European recognition of the secessionist South in the American Civil War.[58] Like the declaration made by Rousseau's censor concerning the cowardice of seconds in duels, such recognition was both denotative and performative; it served not only to categorize antagonists, but also to amplify a combination of motives and capacities already in play, with significant practical effects.

In a later article, written in 1953, Schmitt extends his etymology of *nomos* along the lines established in *Land and Sea*, where it designates a fundamental combination of appropriation, distribution, and production (seizure, dividing, and tending) that defines every sociopolitical order.[59] Signifying all these dimensions, *nomos* traverses politics, society, and culture. "Abstractly speaking, *nomos* is law and property. . . . Concretely speaking, *nomos* is, for example, the chicken in every pot that every peasant living under a good king has on Sunday . . . and the car that every American worker has parked in his garage."[60] However, *nomos* is not simply a substrate worked up by any *-cracy* or *-archy*. Rather, "*nomos* penetrates *archy* and *cracy*. Neither can exist without *nomos*."[61] As he puts it, *nomos* serves as the "immanent measure" of planning and administration, without which the latter become spaceless planning of raw material.[62]

Nomos thus signifies everything, and every substantial relationship among things, disregarded by legal formalism. Schmitt traces the latter—embodied in positive law—back to the earliest forgettings of acquisition, the first stabilizations of territory in the transition from nomadic to fixed households.[63]

> After the land-appropriating and land-division have been completed, when the problems of founding anew and of transition have been surpassed, and some degree of calculability and security have been achieved, the word *nomos* acquires another meaning. The epoch of constituting quickly is forgotten or, more often, becomes a semi-conscious matter. The *situation établie* of those constituted dominates all customs, as well as all thought and speech. Normativism and positivism then become the most plausible and self-evident matters in the world, especially where there is no longer any horizon other than the *status quo*.[64]

Among the substantial conditions of lawfulness sublimated by the abstraction of *nomos* as norm or law, Schmitt includes "passion."[65] As we have seen, this was the last vestige of form underlying political distinctions following the dissolution of a stable Catholic ethos, comprising the "substantial" ground for national sovereignty embodied in a charismatic executive. Forgotten in a global normativism and positivism, deterritorialized passions would contribute to the unraveling of European *nomos*. Yet—as we shall see—they would continue to gather around key figures such as the partisan, the territorial delimitation of which would become Schmitt's great concern.

Globalization and the Dissolution of the *Jus Publicum Europaeum*

Grounded in a multivalent and fluid substrate, a flexible *status quo* "stronger than any legitimacy or even legality," European international law was able to bracket conflict among nations even in times of transformation. Nonetheless, the elastic composition of order and positioning had its breaking point. As Schmitt wrote earlier, "In the history of political ideas, there are epochs of great energy and times becalmed, times of motionless status quo."[66]

The main vector of European dissolution was the globalization of trade. However, just as the *Jus Publicum Europaeum* was composed of a complex of overlapping orders, its dissolution was the work of a combination of factors undermining the territorial integrity of the European state system at the end of the nineteenth century. Among them, Schmitt includes the entry of Japan as a great power, the closing of European colonization in the Americas and emergence of a western power-bloc with the Monroe doctrine, the expansion and intensification of industrialization, and the technological obviation of land and sea divisions by submarine and air power (a subject to which we shall return).

In concert, these developments dissolved the ground from beneath international law, which was extended to non-European states lacking a "spatial or spiritual consciousness" in which even "civilization could no longer provide any concrete hegemony."[67] Without a foundation in customary modes of reciprocity, recognition among nations lost its constitutive effect and became a mere formality. International agreements were reduced to a voluntary "certification of trust."[68] Among the signs of this turn was Belgium's claim to the Congo by virtue of "effective occupation," that is, on the basis of tenuous facts of power rather than the legal recognition of a European order defined as the "sacral center" of the earth and secured by the Great Powers.[69] "The belief in civilization and progress had become nothing more than an ideological façade. . . . Essentially, the whole enterprise already was a helpless confusion of lines dividing spheres of interest and influence, as well as of failed amity lines simultaneously overarched and undermined by a Eurocentrically conceived, free, global economy ignoring all territorial borders."[70] The new international order rested on a "minimum of constitutional order," namely a shared distinction of the public state from the private economy, a new amity line that "was not a territorial line but rather a line delimiting spheres of human participation."[71] This was a new way of dividing the world, unraveling the coincidence of cultural, economic, legal, and political forms and creating lines of demarcation that cut across national, legal, and cultural spaces. As Schmitt saw it, "the rational relation of norm and exception thereby was reversed."[72] The sovereign maintenance of order gave way to the administration of "confusion," a condition in which, it might be added, we remain today.

Schmitt portrays juridical positivism as blindly complicit in the hollowing of international law. Positivism externalized history and politics, hypostasizing juridical territory and sovereign authority from a complex concrete order.[73] Forgetting the dynamic character of *nomos*, jurists no longer concerned themselves with the relay between legitimacy and mere facts of power.[74] Like the villagers in Gabriel García Márquez's *One Hundred Years of Solitude*, they affixed names to customary objects whose meaning was fading, only to forget how to interpret them. Schmitt laments the loss of even a basic historical sense in positive law, whether national or international. "At the end of the 19th century, jurisprudence, in the name of legal positivism, chose to remain silent with respect to all great contemporaneous legal issues. . . . With this rejection of international law, Europe stumbled into a world war that dethroned the old world from the center of the earth and destroyed the bracketing of war it had created."[75] This indifference to background conditions—the *situation établie*—was characteristic of an "overconfident" late nineteenth century.[76] Thus, even though the collapse of these conditions was signaled in various ways, no one was paying attention. Legal thought in the period externalized not only temporal but also spatial relations, dividing national from international law. "The sharp division of internal and external expressed the state centered thinking of an essentially state-oriented bureaucracy whose thinking dominated public law."[77] In particular, legal thinkers focused on tensions between inside and outside, state and international law, while overlooking the significance of the divide between economic globalism and political pluralism. "Precisely here—in the economy—the old spatial order of the earth lost its structure."[78] The constitutive origins of the *situation établie* were forgotten, and the mediation of order and orientation was replaced by a proliferation of legislative enactments and Caesaristic attempts at direct control.[79] The global war that resulted was characterized by a confused blend of national alliances and international norms, feudal tactics, and modern weapons, and the end of the *Jus Publicum Europaeum*.

Schmitt's condemnation of the doomed Treaty of Versailles and the League of Nations centers on their failure to constitute a new *nomos* in place of the old. "The essential cause of the failure of the League was that it lacked any decision with respect to, or even any idea of a spatial order."[80] Faced with the alternative of global sovereignty or a pluralism of federated *Grossräume* based on a balance between Europe and the rest of the Western Hemisphere, the League instead produced a confused blend of national sovereignty and economic globalism, interstate agreements and universal norms.[81] The result, in any case, was an exacerbated split between form and substance. Out of the postwar international conferences and conventions, two general doctrines emerged whose combination formed a fatal contradiction: just war, and global free trade. While the notion of just war rendered the spatial *status quo* absolute, outlawing political land appropriation as such, free trade and economic pressures (e.g., those exercised by the United States) wreaked havoc on the internal constitution of supposedly sovereign states. *Political space was reduced to a positive status quo while the substance corresponding to that order was eroded by flows of industry, finance, and labor.*[82] The resulting social instability was compounded, in the case of Germany, by economic sanctions based on the new, discriminatory conception of just war, retrospectively designating Germany a criminal aggressor state. Schmitt specifically mentions the disregard in the Paris Peace for the stability of a national currency.[83]

In *Land and Sea*, Schmitt emphasizes the role of British maritime power, which had been the primary agent of global free trade, and the first world power in one element.[84] However, in *Nomos*, Schmitt argues it was the United States that formalized the bifurcation of political and socioeconomic space, reserving the right to influence nations whose territorial integrity it simultaneously sanctified.[85] "The United States believed it could turn the political into an external façade of territorial borders, that it could transcend territorial borders with the essential content of the economic. But, in a decisive moment, it was unable to prevent the political grouping of friend and enemy from becoming critical."[86] While critical of inconsistent and hypocritical applications of free-trade doctrines—compromised as always by various protectionist measures and privileged partnerships—Schmitt focuses his attack on the new formulations of just war, which he depicted as a threat not only to Germany but the world as a whole. He traces the legal transformations toward a criminalization of war from Versailles, through the failed Geneva Protocol of 1924, to the genuine transformation achieved with the "renunciation of war as an instrument of national policy" in the Kellogg Pact in 1928. Legal scholars conceptualized the new approach to war by way of a modern reformulation of scholastic notions, specifically that formulated by Francisco de Vitoria in the sixteenth century. In the hands of James Brown Scott, specifically, Vitoria's concepts of reciprocity and humanity were "instrumentalized" (stripped of their theological and institutional suppositions) in humanitarian arguments that asserted freedom of secular trade and propaganda, and criminalized military responses.[87] Although justified in Vitoria's terms, modern just war doctrine departs from medieval formulas that sanctified aggressive war as a theological mission authorized by the institutional authority of the Church. While rejecting historical or biological arguments that de-humanized the colonized peoples, Schmitt emphasizes, Vitoria had nonetheless approved the Spanish conquest as a kind of "humanitarian intervention" against those refusing "free" commerce and religious propaganda (thus appealing to the conversion rather than the absolute subjugation of indigenous populations).[88] Rather than a "neutral" response to unlawful aggression on the part of the indigenous population, however, conquest was justified by the papal missionary mandate.[89]

The new conception of just war differs from both ecumenical and stat-
ist predecessors while drawing on both, combining the language of just war
while evacuating its theological, Eurocentric, and institutional underpin-
nings. Rather than a return to an earlier global order, the new doctrine of
just war signals a "fundamental transformation."[90]

> In the modern, discriminatory concept of war, the distinction between the
> justice and injustice of war makes the enemy a felon, who no longer is treated
> as a *justus hostis*, but as a criminal. Consequently, war ceases to be a matter of
> international law, even if the killing, plundering and annihilation continue
> and intensify with new, modern means of destruction. . . . This may be a return
> to an older standpoint. In some respects, however, it also is a retreat from the
> juridical concept of *justus hostis* to a quasi-theological concept of the enemy.
> In any case, it is the antithesis of a non-discriminatory reciprocity taken to its
> extreme, which Vitoria expresses in a clearly Christian sense.[91]

Like its medieval precursor, modern "just war" doctrine deprives the an-
tagonist of equivalent legal status. However, combines with the rationality
and means proper to the secular police state, which further depoliticizes the
enemy, and reduces justice to a kind of "social pest control" [*Schädlingsbekäm-
fung*].[92]

As noted earlier, the legal collapse of territorial reciprocity coincides with
new military technologies that enhance the physical violence of conflict,
transcend territorial boundaries, and contribute to the de-humanization of
the enemy. Most crucially, the purely destructive mode of warfare proper to
air power requires no occupying force and therefore no direct *contact* with
the other that might lead to legal and customary ties. A precedent for such
violence was the "prize war" formerly isolated to the free seas. "A blockad-
ing fleet has only a negative relation to enemy territory and its inhabitants,
because it considers both the land and the people to be nothing more than
the goal of a forceful action and the object of a means of compulsion."[93] Air
war produces a more thorough deterritorialization, a "structural transformation" of human topography and an "absolute" disconnection from the enemy
population. "Not even the shadow of a relation between protection and
obedience remains. Independent air war allows neither the one nor the other
side a possibility to establish a relation."[94] In the elemental sense Schmitt im-
parts to the term, air power—which he associates not only with aircraft but
also electronic waves that traverse the globe[95]—destroys the old opposition
of land and sea, and with them the boundaries of order and chaos, soldier and
civilian. It culminates a shift toward abstract "geometrical" space that began
with the introduction of political space to the sea in the Monroe Doctrine.

With the conquest of the skies and the view from above, we might say political space took on the "intellectual" quality attributed to it by Bergson. As Schmitt puts it in *Land and Sea*, "Space has become the field of man's energy, activity and creativity . . . 'it is not the world that is in space, but rather, it is space that is in the world.'"[96] Freed from the fixed spaces of legal and territorial integrity, the new technologies of politics promised a mastery of spatial becoming, a "real-time" fluid sovereignty.[97] Of course, Schmitt was hardly reconciled to the collapse of territorial boundaries and political distinctions.[98] Nor was this the result of the developments he described. Following the carnage of World War II, the Eurocentric order gave way to a new division of the earth between West and East, after a brief unification in 1945.[99] Nonetheless, when Schmitt completed *Nomos* in 1950 it remained to be seen what political order, or lack thereof, would emerge from the combination of geostrategic realignments, nuclear weapons, accelerated national economies, and new technologies of communication and propaganda. In his conclusions, Schmitt considers three possible forms a new *nomos* might take. The first would be the triumph of either east or west, resulting in a single, global sovereign. "The victor . . . would appropriate the whole earth—land, sea, and air—and would divide and manage it in accord with his plans and ideas."[100] He treats this possibility as a technological fantasy, albeit one encouraged by the very real shrinking of space. "The existence of modern technology should neither make us drunk nor lead us to despair. We need neither abandon human reason nor cease to consider rationally all the possibilities of a new *nomos* of the earth."[101] Schmitt considers two alternatives. First is a return to a balance of states, with the United States taking over the proper role of the *Katechon*—a role played by the Christian empire in the Middle Ages, and briefly attempted by Britain—enforcing the freedom not only of the sea but also of airspace; second, "a combination of several independent *Grossräume* could constitute a balance, and thereby could precipitate a new order of the earth." The latter option, while more novel, would be "rational, if the *Grossräume* are differentiated meaningfully and are homogeneous internally."[102] He declines to predict which order will ultimately prevail.

Theorizing the Partisan: Philosophy, Technology, and the Dislocation of Enmity

The *nomos* of the Cold War combined nuclear "balance" with bloody proxy-wars and a variety of anticolonial struggles for national self-determination. In this context, Schmitt revisited the themes of *The Nomos of the Earth*, linking them to the problem of the enemy established in *The Concept of the Political*.

In *Theory of the Partisan: Intermediate Commentary on the Concept of the Political* (1963), he places the partisan at the center of changing modes of warfare, politics, enmity, and territoriality. In the emergence of the partisan as a philosophically and legally recognized figure, he finds signs of both the collapse of a "telluric" order and the last possibility for its persistence. Schmitt initially defines the partisan by three criteria: "*Irregularity* (non-uniformed fighters); increased *mobility* (or 'flexibility') of active combat; and increased *intensity* of political engagement."[103] He then adds a fourth criterion that distinguishes the "true" partisan, who is *telluric* in nature, that is, part of an autochthonous group engaged in a defensive struggle against a foreign power. For Schmitt, this true partisan serves as the last outpost of territorial (bracketed) struggle, beyond which lies a radical destruction of political form. He writes, "[the partisan] deforms his nature when he appropriates absolute and technicized aggressivity or dreams about a world revolution."[104]

We can pause here to note the conjunction of technological and ideological deformity in Schmitt's formulations, anticipating further discussion of their relationship below. Schmitt's discussion of *nomos* suggests an interplay between our tools and our dreams that complicates both moralism and instrumentalism. We have already encountered some examples of this interplay. On one hand, moral righteousness intensifies violence in a "gruesome" way. Yet, on the other, air power contributes to the de-humanization of the enemy, and even calls forth moral absolutism. The discovery of the New World—which for Schmitt inaugurated a new *nomos* with all its attendant legal and moral significance—also stemmed from a combination of global imaginaries and naval innovations. As I argue later, similar entanglements lead to a confusion of the authentic and the deformed partisan, and ultimately complicate the relationship between its theory and practice.

The modern partisan originated in the Spanish Civil War, a guerilla war waged against organized Napoleonic forces. Although mobile troops who did not fight in regular formation were not in themselves new, the partisan forces that emerged in this conflict were not the light combat units of previous eras, which had merely supplemented regular armies. Still, while the Spanish fighters establish the criteria outlined above, the partisan only gradually became a legal and conceptual figure. Schmitt traces the arc along which this figure emerges, beginning with a "spark" in the Spanish Civil War that flies to Germany, catches fire with Prussian philosophy, and is then transmitted by Clausewitz to Lenin and Mao. Along this arc, one finds, first, a philosophical legitimation of partisanship, second, (failed) attempts at its legal circumscription (i.e., Geneva 1949),[105] and, finally, a shift in the nature of the partisan as such, from the defender of a national territory to the agent of world revolution. In this final turn, the basis of partisan struggle shifts from (authentic) concrete territoriality to abstract ideas, that is, from nation to class, and from a defensive to an aggressive posture. In Schmitt's new terms, the former struggle is waged against a "real" and the latter against an "absolute" enemy. The former need only be repelled, the latter destroyed by any means necessary.

Summarized this way, the historical development of the partisan reverses the territorialization of global class hostilities achieved by nationalism as Schmitt described it in *The Crisis of Parliamentary Democracy*. It springs from much the same decentering of conflict that appears in *The Concept of the Political*. As indicated by the etymology of the term, the intensity of political engagement that distinguishes the irregularity of the partisan from a mere criminal or individualistic rebel is associated not with a state but a party affiliation.[106] The partisan's mobility, in turn, results from the technological "motorization" of war that undermines the territorial logic of the old land wars. As Clausewitz wrote earlier, "a popular uprising should, in general, be considered as an outgrowth of the way in which the conventional barriers have been swept away in our lifetime by the elemental violence of war."[107] As we have seen, mobility and intensity are interrelated. As in *The Nomos of the Earth*, the dislocation of struggle also undermines the bracketing of violence, blurring distinctions between soldier and civilian, war and peace. "By comparison with a war of absolute enmity, the bracketed war of traditional European international law that flowed within well defined banks following known rules is nothing more than a duel between gentlemen seeking satisfaction."[108] Partisan wars leave no place for gentlemen, as regular armies must adapt to the tactics of their opponents, resulting in a cycle of "terror and counter-terror."[109] While partisan war thus shares many aspects of sea war, Schmitt withdrew his earlier description of the pirate as a "partisan of the sea."[110] The fourth, telluric criterion that distinguishes the true partisan thus becomes crucial, as it is the basis for a potential last stand, of sorts, that is, for an attempt to circumscribe this figure—and with it the modern warfare it signifies—within a bounded order.

As Rodolphe Gasché argues, citing Munkler, the partisan is an ambiguous figure, "functioning either as a renewer or destroyer of the state."[111] In Schmitt's terms, we might say he or she can be either a *Katechon* or an *Archeront*, a force of territorialized or unbounded hostility.[112] Historically, this ambiguity is illustrated by the fact that Clausewitz's formulation of war as a continuation of politics—which for Schmitt "contains the Theory of the Partisan in a nutshell"—was interpreted in the revolutionary-absolute direction by Lenin and the limited, telluric one by Mao (Gasché does not mention Schmitt's inclusion of Stalin in the latter category). As Gasché demonstrates, furthermore, both possibilities were already present discursively (*in nuce*) in Clausewitz's text, which distinguishes between different types of politics of which war can be a continuation. In the first, war is simply another means to realize limited, concrete goals that are also pursued by other political means. It is thus limited by instrumental calculations of interest and reward. However, in the second, a different kind of war follows the "grand and powerful" politics of revolutionary France, in which enmity takes an absolute form associated with Enlightenment ideals, making peace undistinguishable from war.[113] Gasché asks:

> What, then, is it that predisposes the philosophical consecration of the genuine partisan to grow into the aggressive world-revolutionary, and thus to destabilize the figure of the authentic partisan? What is it that, within philosophy and its legitimization of the partisan's struggle against the real enemy, leads to a founding philosophy of absolute hostility? If the notion of revolutionary civil war originates in seeds planted in Clausewitz's theory of war, this is a seed that undoubtedly, from the beginning, makes the ideal type of the partisan a shaky concept. However, what becomes clear as well is that, without the construct of a genuine partisan, there is no hope whatsoever for a containment of enmity, and hence of politics as such.[114]

Gasché thus seeks a decisive transformation of hostility in philosophy. He concludes:

> The statement that "war is a continuation of politics" houses, indeed, the seed of partisan theory, one that is capable of accounting in fact for the chameleon-like character of the partisan. It is a statement that lends itself both to a political conception of the genuine, or true, partisan, and an abstract-philosophical conception of him as the "authentic irregular." The seed of the partisan, however, is primarily philosophical. He is born from philosophy—from a philosophy in the spirit of the Enlightenment, which spiritually consecrates him as the fighter of an absolute enmity in the name of just causes. By contrast, the political interpretation of the partisan, even though it is also influenced by philosophy, seeks, at its own risk, to trim the seedling by imposing clear distinctions on this figure, so as to contain it within the bounds of policy and real, rather than abstract, causes. In contrast with the absolute and pure concepts of philosophy, those by way of which the philosophical seedling is made to grow into a figure of the political lack the reliability and stability of such pure conceptions. They are tentative, always threatened by the failure to contain absolute enmity and to secure an order of the political. Therefore, political theory's decision to rely on these distinc-

tions, or criteria, for mastering the ambiguous phenomenon of the partisan also takes place only at its own risk.[115]

As Gasché understands, one cannot easily isolate philosophical and political sources of enmity.[116] As he describes it, the move from philosophy to politics involves both clarification and destabilization. "Pure concepts of philosophy" only yield clear distinctions when trimmed and planted in the soil of politics. However, the political development of the philosophical seed *lacks* "the stability of such pure conceptions." Clarity and stability, then, are at odds at the intersection of different media. This much I have already noted. The discursive stability of positive law, for example, depends upon an extra-legal stability, and leads to confusion when superimposed on abnormal conditions. Contrarily, personal representation, as we saw earlier, achieves stability by fusing a plurality of associations in a vague, flexible combination of opposites. However, the relative stability or clarity of a given discourse is not easy to determine, as both law and authority rest on complex processes of mediation. Philosophical *figures*, Gasché writes, are "shaky" carriers of intensities emitted from social and political struggles. Yet intensities can also stabilize a discourse around nodal points or polemical oppositions. Latent contradictions within Enlightenment ideals, for example, were subsumed by a polemical orientation to monarchy. Furthermore, it was the polemical struggle of Spanish partisans against Napoleon, recall, that gave rise to "sparks" that only later become "explosive" when gathered and catalyzed by Lenin's philosophy.[117] Earlier, we saw how Marx's philosophy channeled a plurality of struggles in a single (class) opposition to the figure of the bourgeois. Every situation is itself composed of an internally dynamic combination of forces, including discursive practice. In *The Nomos of the Earth*, similarly, Schmitt links *topos* to the agora, and to rhetoric, the public counterpart of academic dialectic.[118] Space and language, context and content, in short, are mutually constitutive.

Ultimately, attempts to isolate a figure or concept from the medium in which it develops are misleading. Philosophical "seeds" are not merely trimmed, but arise in the soil of politics, in the form of polemical energies, or spacks, prior to their consecration.[119] Perhaps these form what Schmitt calls the "ghost of an idea" in *Roman Catholicism and Political Form*.[120] As he did in that earlier text, Schmitt describes a staged process whereby concrete differences are assembled, abstracted, and idealized followed by a subsequent concrete delimitation of the resulting figure. The concrete individuals subsumed under the sign of this figure become participants in an ideal (or spiritual) order. In the terms Schmitt developed in *Roman Catholicism and Political Form*, they harbor a common essence or idea that can be "represented," regardless of their positive differentiation. Since an abstract figure is not reducible to a given set of concrete individuals it conflates and combines; its application to new cases is ultimately a political, rather than merely logical process. Nor, however, is it wholly arbitrary. As Schmitt shows, the nature of this application is shaped by the intensities carried over from the plurality of conflicts out of which the figure arises.

This mutually constitutive interaction of philosophical and political figures is illustrated in Schmitt's discussion of the "accreditation" of the partisan as a revolutionary figure in Prussia. The Enlightenment philosophy taken up by Fichte, as well as "highly educated and brilliant military men" including Clausewitz, did not invent but "discovered" this figure. "In such an atmosphere, in which an aroused national feeling [erregtes National-algefühl] blended itself [sich. . . vereinigte] with a philosophical education, philosophy discovered the partisan, thus making it a theoretical elaboration."[121]

> If Fichte's early project of a closed commercial state in which humanity would achieve absolute freedom implied a great number of concrete enemies—the sovereigns, the nobility, the church, the Jews, and the military (both of whom [sic] Fichte considered as states within the state)—"one great enemy," namely, Napoleon, replaced them all after 1807. "All the enmity of which the revolutionary philosopher is capable, became concentrated from that moment on against the French emperor, and became manifest in the latter's figure . . . Fichte is the proper [eigentlicher] philosopher of enmity against Napoleon. One can say that he is this philosopher of enmity in his very existence as a philosopher."[122]

Once again, the symbolic concentration of friend and enemy channels polemical intensities. Yet these intensities are not organic, but (also) symbolically "educated." The philosophical recognition of the partisan (expressed in the Prussian edic of 1813 that mandated resistance to Napoleon on the part of all citizens, and by any means) drew on the dissemination of partisan spirit in popular literature. In particular Schmitt mentions the role of publicists in Austria, including Friedrich Genz and Friedrich Schlegel, who translated and published anti-Napoleonic Spanish pamphlets in 1809, seeking to incite the same spirit of partisan struggle.[123] Heinrich von Kleist expanded on their efforts, becoming a "poet of national resistance."[124] As Schmitt argues, the intensity of political engagement proper to party or partisan affiliation had diverse sources that blend and give rise to an existential or absolute hostility in revolutionary times, when "a very general and ambiguous designation can suddenly become profoundly political."[125] We should remember here that a political status for the partisan is tied to the notion of legitimacy. The "Partisan has an absolute need for legitimation if he is to remain in the political sphere, and not simply sink into that of a common criminal."[126] Unlike the Catholic combination of opposites, which rested on a gradual process of mediation in which all parts were consecrated, the concentration of profane sentiments here is "sudden," or even "explosive." Conversely, the radical implications of Fichte's philosophy of the partisan were quickly dampened when circumstances changed. Schmitt writes:

> The Archeront that had broken the banks for a little while immediately re-entered within the framework of state order. After the wars of liberation, Hegel's philosophy became dominant in Prussia. It sought a systematic mediation of revolution and tradition. It was considered a conservative philosophy, and it undoubtedly was. But it also succeeded in retaining the revolutionary spark, and through its interpretation of history it provided a dangerous ideological weapon, even more dangerous than Rousseau's philosophy in the Jacobin's hands.[127]

As the final sentence of Schmitt's text attests, theory plays a major role in the development of the partisan. Yet absolute enmity does not follow from philosophy *per se*, but from a fertile combination of concepts and circumstances. Returning to the recurrent figure of confluence, Schmitt concludes, "The theory of the Partisan flows into [*mündet*] the concept of the political, into the question concerning who is the real enemy and in a new *nomos* of the earth."[128] Discourse, or rhetoric (as we saw earlier) shapes, directs, and amplifies what it purports to describe. Similarly, we saw how the recognition of great powers contributed to the force of insurgencies.[129] Like Marx's image of the bourgeois, the theoretical figure of the partisan blends with a larger stream of habits, affections, and ideas, gathering "sparks" of conflict that float along like half-submerged mines.[130]

Gasché's question regarding the origins of absolute enmity must therefore be revised. One should not seek them in philosophy *per se*. Where else, then, can we look? Among the factors radicalizing the partisan, technology figures prominently. In *The Nomos of the Earth*, Schmitt had already recognized the importance of technological advances in transportation and warfare that transformed relations between friend and enemy. Schmitt's discussion of air war indicates the central role of technological innovations generally in the historical transformation of *nomos*. In *Land and Sea*, similarly, the transition from thalassic to oceanic civilization corresponded with the replacement of the oar-propelled galley of Venice to the great sailing fleets. Likewise, the domination of the sea was driven not only by discovery of the New World but new ship-building technology, especially the Dutch invention of the square sail, "the great turning point in the history of the relationship between land and sea."[131] The deterritorialization accomplished by air power was also predated by the invention of broadside naval cannon fire, the beginning of authentic naval combat (not involving hand-to-hand fighting).[132] In each case, normative and juridical realignments follow technological developments. For example, piracy becomes criminal activity in an era of scientific-industrial shipping.[133]

None of this is to suggest some kind of technological determinism on Schmitt's part. As he notes elsewhere, the technological obviation of *de facto* spatial boundaries is not enough to explain changing legal forms. After all, the traditional three-mile boundary persisted long after having been rendered symbolic by enhanced artillery. Along similar lines, he cites Hegel's and Marx's arguments regarding the "artificially prolonged virginity" of economic freedom that persisted after the American frontier no longer provided an outlet for political conflict among different religious and economic groupings.[134] Technology, for Schmitt, is always part of an interactive process. Both in *The Nomos of the Earth* and *Theory of the Partisan*, he suggests humanity "needs" concepts of just war to legitimate the intensified violence of weapons of mass destruction.[135] As he explains, "the present weapons of total mass destruction or men's premeditated evil do not constitute the ultimate danger. Rather, the danger lies in the inescapability of a moral obligation. Those men who use these weapons against other men feel compelled to destroy these other men, i.e., their victims, even morally."[136]

If we commit too much violence against them, we cannot bear the reproach of our victims. Thus, Bodin's salutary demoralization of war is reversed by the machine gun. Yet this very possibility reveals another reversal. Absolute enmity has become the consequence rather than the cause of spectacular violence. Or, rather, neither technology (weapons of mass destruction) nor human nature (premeditated evil) can be isolated as sources of absolute enmity, or even as independent qualities. In *The Theory of the Partisan*, Schmitt writes, "It goes without saying that, in concrete reality, there are no isolated and independent aspects, but that only their respective relations and their functional dependence produce a general picture. . . . Ultimately, they all end up falling within the force-field of a technological-industrial development. . . . The technological enhancement of human technological efficiency shatters entire normative systems."[137] Similarly, the partisan is "uprooted from his environment" by his technological "motorization."[138] Again, none of this is to suggest that Schmitt had succumbed to determinism, though his resistance sometimes has a wistful quality, as when he warns against the progressive technocratic ideology that imagines the partisan "will disappear simply of his own accord, within smooth technological-functional processes, just as a dog disappears from the freeway."[139] In a sense, technology takes the place occupied by nature in *Land and Sea*, determining "not only [Man's] horizon . . . but also his poise, his movements, his figure and his height" yet without leaving him "a creature wholly conditioned by his medium."[140]

Schmitt's task, once again, was to contain material forces of destruction. "Enmity and war are inevitable. What counts is their containment, that is, preventing that the means of destruction resulting from the scientific process are unleashed in inhuman ways."[141] The basis of this containment, however, is uncertain. As we have seen, the picture of a struggle between material forces and philosophical or political categories falsifies their practical interpenetration. New technologies change not only the means but also the aim, scope, and justifications of conflict. Moreover, they change the significance of political theory.

Schmitt was acutely aware that the circulation of scholarly concepts in unpredictable discursive contexts—made possible by modern media technologies—can contribute to powerful realignments. In his trial at Nuremberg, facing accusations of contributing to the Nazi regime, he argues the following:

Theories and ideas do have influence, but this influence is not traceable to "decisive points." The effects of spoken, written and printed words are various and incalculable. . . . In times of peace and security, specialists in such disciplines are allowed the greatest freedom of thought and are not troubled with the question of the possible effects of their opinions. In times of open or latent civil war, there is the danger that every open and public word will at once be changed into a propaganda slogan or fall victim to the nihilistic chaos of ravaged concepts. . . . Translated into the language of modern technology, one might formulate this experience in the following way: Every amplification is a change of meaning and usually also a falsification of it. . . . The question becomes not simpler but more difficult in an age of technology and mass communication, because it is linked with a special power factor—the psycho-technical machinery of modern propaganda, whose loudspeakers can make or break myths from day to day. Once warned, it was precisely this amplification that I sought to avoid.[142]

In this passage, Schmitt alternately describes and rhetorically enacts the confluence of technology and discourse that forms the partisan. At the same time, he undermines his earlier depiction of the decision, moving in a more plausible, albeit self-serving, direction. No longer are there decisive points that stand apart from complex processes, whether politically or discursively. Yet there are still thresholds of more or less radical change. As we saw previously, modern political affiliations are not drawn strictly from shared norms or voluntary ties based on objective interests, but also from combinations of ideas, habits, and affections forged by mobilizing images. Schmitt thus reiterates the complex relationship between theory and political struggles outlined earlier, whereby ideas amplify and combine political interests and conflicts. He also confirms the acceleration of political representation, from a more or less continuous ethos of belief, tied to traditional symbols, to a mobile, eruptive pathos channeled by "day to day" myths. In *Theory of the Partisan*, he describes the emergence of partisan groupings not in terms of confluence and channeling but sparks and explosions, indicating an accelerated dislocation of politics akin to that described in *The Concept of the Political*. Combined with new weaponry, the catalytic intensification of political affiliations poses the threat of new kinds of mushrooms. However, as Schmitt discovered too late, attempts to preempt them pose their own grave dangers.

Notes

1. On Schmitt's role in the Nazi administration, see Joseph Bendersky, *Carl Schmitt: Theorist for the Reich* (Princeton, NJ: Princeton University Press, 1983) part IV.

2. On Schmitt's trial, see Joseph Bendersky, "Carl Schmitt at Nuremberg," *Telos* 72 (Summer 1987): 91–129.

3. Cf. Franz Neumann, *Behemoth* (New York: Harper and Row, 1944), chapter 5; Ellen Kennedy, *Constitutional Failure, Carl Schmitt in Weimar* (Durham, NC: Duke University Press, 2004), 28; Bendersky, *Carl Schmitt*, 252–53. Kennedy contrasts Schmitt's turn toward a "concrete order" with Popitz's insistence on the priority of the state as the basis of political unity. On Schmitt's defense against charges of developing the term to justify Hitler's expansionist policies, see Bendersky, "Carl Schmitt at Nuremberg," 107–8.

4. Carl Schmitt. *The Nomos of the Earth*, trans. G. L. Ulmen (New York: Telos Press, 2003), 66, hereafter *Nomos*.

5. Carl Schmitt. *Land and Sea*, trans. Simona Draghici (Corvallis, OR: Plutarch Press, 1997), hereafter, *LS*.

6. See Carl Schmitt, *Theory of the Partisan*, trans. G. L. Ulmen, *Telos* 127 (Spring 2004): 11–78.

7. Jan-Werner Müller thus describes Schmitt's writings from this period as a return to conservatism following his disastrous complicity with a radicalization of the exception in Hitler's rule by decree. Cf. Müller, *A Dangerous Mind* (New Haven, CT: Yale University Press, 2003), 46. On the notion of the *Katechon*, see Schmitt, *Nomos*, 59–66. Schmitt describes the Christian Middle Ages as a struggle *for* Rome, a concrete empire rather than abstract norms, and hence for the continuity of a given historical "eon," which is maintained by restraining the antichrist. He also refers the "*Katechon*, i.e., a monarchy grounded in a country and its people." Schmitt, *Nomos*, 64.

8. Schmitt, *Nomos*, 70. Schmitt's etymology is sometimes considered idiosyncratic or suspect. Distribution or allocation, rather than "appropriation" or "taking," are more common translations of *Nemein*. *Nomos* is also translated as "pasture, district, custom, law." Cf. Kypros.org at www.kypros.org/cgi-bin/lexicon. Heidegger provides the following definition: "In Greek, to assign is *nemein*. *Nomos* is not only law but more originally the assignment contained in the dispensation of Being. Only the assignment is capable of dispatching man into Being. Only such dispatching is capable of supporting and obligating. Otherwise all law remains merely something fabricated by human reason." Heidegger, "The Letter on Humanism," in *Basic Writings*, ed. David Farrel Krell (New York: Harper Collins, 1993), 262. Quoted in Christopher Fynsk, "A Nomos without Truth," *South Atlantic Quarterly* 104.2 (Spring 2005): 317, n. 7. Compare: "The Greek word for law, nomos, derives from nemein, which means to distribute, to possess (what has been distributed), and to dwell. The combination of law and hedge in the word nomos is quite manifest in a fragment from Heraclitus . . . 'the people should fight for the law as for a wall.'" Hannah Arendt, *The Human Condition* (Chicago: University of Chicago Press, 1958), 63.

9. See Niccolò Machiavelli, "Discourses," in *Selected Political Writings*, ed. David Wooton (Indianapolis, IN: Hackett, 1994), 85.

10. Schmitt, *PT*, 13; Schmitt, *Nomos*, 81–82.

11. Schmitt, *Nomos*, 71. See also 248 on a status quo with no "unifying principle."

12. Schmitt, *Nomos*, 74.

13. Schmitt, *Nomos*, 73. Cf. Schmitt, *Der Nomos der Erde im Volkerrecht des Jus Publicum Europaeum* (Berlin: Duncker & Humblot, 1997), 42.

14. See Schmitt, *Nomos*, 327, fn. 5.

15. "Ortung," which has a nautical history and is linked to various notions of locality (as in "*Ort*," a town or place), has of late been adopted for new technologies, namely "global positioning systems." Cf. LEO GmbH Deutsch-English Wörterbuch, //dict.leo.org/?lang=de. Müller translates *Ortung* as "localization," thus capturing its active quality, a choice I follow here. Cf. Jan-Werner Müller, *A Dangerous Mind*, 88.

16. Schmitt, *Nomos*, 74.

17. Schmitt, *Nomos*, 58.

18. Schmitt, *Nomos*, 59–64.

19. Schmitt, *Nomos*, 59.

20. In *Land and Sea*, Schmitt notes the brutality visited by European colonial forces one upon the other. However, one distinction remained between these enemies and the colonized. The accusation of cannibalism was reserved for the latter. See Schmitt, *LS*, 40.

21. Schmitt, *Nomos*, 95.

22. Schmitt, *Nomos*, 92.

23. Schmitt follows Hobbes and Locke in this respect, depicting indigenous Americans as lawless savages. He acknowledged, however, the centrality of domination involved. "One might as well and more correctly define the age of discoveries as the era of territorial conquests by the Europeans." Schmitt, *LS*, 40.

24. Schmitt, *Nomos*, 199.

25. Cf. Schmitt, *Nomos*, 59, 92, 186.

26. See Otto Brunner, *Land and Lordship*, trans. Howard Kaminsky and James Van Horn Melton (Philadelphia: University of Pennsylvania Press, 1992). Kennedy points out that Brunner had himself been influenced by Schmitt's *Concept of the Political*. Cf. Kennedy, *Constitutional Failure*, 29.

27. Schmitt, *Nomos*, 141–43, 186.

28. See Schmitt, *CP*, 28–29. Rodolphe Gasché sees Schmitt's conception of "bracketed enmity" in *The Nomos of the Earth* as directly following from *The Concept of the Political*. See Gasché, "The Partisan and the Philosopher," *South Atlantic Quarterly* 104.2 (Spring 2005): 9–34.

29. Schmitt, *Nomos*, 156–57. See also Schmitt, *PT*, 8–9, where Schmitt credits Bodin for having linked the abstract notion of sovereignty as the "highest power" to the concrete problem of the decision. Schmitt also links this continuity to the notion of a provisional state of exception in *Nomos*, 209.

30. Schmitt, *Nomos*, 166.

31. Schmitt, *Nomos*, 188.

32. Cf. Schmitt, *Nomos*, 320–21.

33. See Schmitt, *Nomos*, 185–86. See also 310.

34. Schmitt, *Nomos*, 157–58. See also 186.

35. On Schmitt's critique of "just" war, see also Schmitt, *CP*, 49.

36. Schmitt, *Nomos*, 168.

37. Schmitt, *Nomos*, 187.

38. Schmitt, *Nomos*, 202.

39. Cf. Schmitt, *Nomos*, 198, 203.

40. Schmitt, *Nomos*, 204.

41. See G. W. F. Hegel, *Philosophy of Right*, trans. T. M. Knox (New York: Oxford University Press, 1952), par. 324.

42. See Frederic Jameson, "Notes on Nomos," *South Atlantic Quarterly* 104.2 (Spring 2005): 199–204, 200. This judgment might seem to receive ample support in *Land and Sea*, where Schmitt posits a change in spatial orientation more fundamental than any particular material, scientific, or artistic discovery of new lands, spaces, and perspectives. See Schmitt, *LS*, 35–36. However, he treats all these elements not as

symptoms of some spiritual transformation, but also as sources for it. See also *LS*, 37: "all manifestations of man's creative genius, the arts, science and technology had their share in the new idea of space."

43. Schmitt, *Nomos*, 186.

44. Schmitt, *Nomos*, 235; Schmitt, *Der Nomos Der Erde*, 208.

45. As Balakrishnan argues, Schmitt's emphasis on land "had nothing to do with the Nazi cult of the soil." Cf. Gopal Balakrishnan, *The Enemy* (New York: Verso, 2000), 250. Jan-Werner Müller also recognizes that Schmitt's conception of *nomos* was "not a mysticism of the soil." Cf. *A Dangerous Mind*, 88. Scheuerman, on the other hand, points to Schmitt's embrace of an organic, racial model of community in his writings during the Nazi period. Scheuerman, *Carl Schmitt*, 164. In his Nazi period, Schmitt described the Jews as "an important cause of the dissolution of concretely-determined territorial orders." Cf. Schmitt, "Völkerrechtliche Grossraumordnung," quoted in Bendersky, "Schmitt at Nuremberg," 100.

46. See Schmitt, *Nomos*, 77–78.

47. Schmitt, *Nomos*, 285.

48. See Schmitt, *Nomos*, 80. In another passage, Schmitt writes, "In no way is the *nomos* limited to the stable and lasting order established by the land-appropriation. On the contrary, it demonstrates its constitutive power in the strongest way possible in the processes that establish order in the original division, the *divisio primaeva*, as noted legal thinkers call it." Schmitt, *Nomos*, 341.

49. Schmitt, *LS*, 36.

50. Cf. Neumann, *Behemoth*, 153.

51. Schmitt, *LS*, 32.

52. Christopher Fynsk reduces Schmitt's conception of *nomos*, alternately describing it as an "abstract" view of the earth as physical matter and an ontology of "concrete order," which amount to the same thing. This allows him to bring Heideggerian insights to bear against Schmitt. However, as I argue below, Schmitt's account of *nomos* shares much with Heidegger's incorporation of order into an experience of Being characterized by revealing. Cf. Fynsk, "A Nomos without Truth," 314–15.

53. Schwab, *Challenge*, 120.

54. On Merleau-Ponty's similar distinction between "geometrical" space and "anthropological space," see Michel de Certeau, *The Practice of Everyday Life* (Berkeley: University of California Press, 1984), 117.

55. Schmitt, *Nomos*, 75. Frederic Jameson traces this critique of abstract space to Husserl. Cf. Jameson, "Notes on Nomos," 200.

56. Jameson, "Notes on Nomos," 167.

57. Jameson, "Notes on Nomos," 303.

58. Jameson, "Notes on Nomos," 300.

59. Cf. Schmitt, "Appropriation/Distribution/Production: An Attempt to Determine from *Nomos* the Basic Questions of Every Social and Economic Order," appended in Schmitt, *Nomos*; Schmitt, *LS*, 37fn.

60. Schmitt, *Nomos*, 327.

61. Schmitt, *Nomos*, 338.

62. Schmitt, *Nomos*, 340.

63. Schmitt, *Nomos*, 341.

64. Schmitt, *Nomos*, 341.

65. Schmitt, *Nomos*, 342.

66. Carl Schmitt, *The Crisis of Parliamentary Democracy*, trans. Ellen Kennedy (Cambridge, MA: MIT Press, 1988), 8.

67. Schmitt, *Nomos*, 234.

68. Schmitt, *Nomos*, 305.

69. Schmitt, *Nomos*, 223.

70. Schmitt, *Nomos*, 226.

71. Schmitt, *Nomos*, 235–36.

72. Schmitt, *Nomos*, 237.

73. Schmitt, *Nomos*, 239. On the similar perspective in economics, see 257. See also Schmitt, *War/Non-War, A Dilemma*, trans. Simona Draghici (Corvallis, OR: Plutarch Press, 2004).

74. Schmitt, *Nomos*, 134.

75. Schmitt, *Nomos*, 239.

76. Schmitt, *Nomos*, 237.

77. Schmitt, *Nomos*, 236.

78. Schmitt, *Nomos*, 237.

79. See Schmitt, *Nomos*, 69–70.

80. Schmitt, *Nomos*, 243. See also Schmitt, *War/Non-War*, 44–45: "the whole order of international law allows itself to be unhinged, yet it creates no new order."

81. On the "indecisive half-measure" of the League Covenant, see Schmitt, *War/Non-War*, 41.

82. See Schmitt, *Nomos*, 235.

83. Schmitt, *Nomos*, 248.

84. See Schmitt, *LS*, 48.

85. See Schmitt, *Nomos*, 252.

86. Schmitt, *Nomos*, 258. Such beliefs, we know, have by no means been vanquished today. Thomas Friedman, for example, has written, "Free Lebanon and free Egypt's economy and they will change the rest of the Middle East for us—for free." Friedman, "New Signs on the Arab Street," *New York Times* online, March 13, 2005, op-ed.

87. Schmitt, *Nomos*, 118–19.

88. Schmitt, *Nomos*, 109. See also Schmitt, *Nomos*, 349.

89. Schmitt, *Nomos*, 112.

90. Schmitt, *Nomos*, 123.

91. Schmitt, *Nomos*, 124.

92. Schmitt, *Nomos*, 125.

93. Schmitt, *Nomos*, 317. Regarding the significance of the blockade, see also Schmitt, *LS*, 47.

94. Schmitt, *Nomos*, 320.

95. See Schmitt, LS, 57–58.

96. Schmitt, LS, 58.

97. "Hence, man's possibilities to dominate nature and his fellow man were given the widest scope." Schmitt, LS, 57. Paul Virilio argues these developments have outstripped space itself as a political category, opening in its place a new "chronopolitics." Cf. Virilio, Speed and Politics, trans. Mark Polizzotti (New York: Semiotext(e), 1986), discussed further in chapter 5. Frederic Jameson emphasizes the emergence of "cyberspace." "Information is the new element that reproblematizes the spatial" to cyberspace. Jameson, "Notes on Nomos," 203–4.

98. In the final passage of Land and Sea, Schmitt writes, "the old nomos is fading away, dragging a whole system of redundant standards, norms and traditions with it, in its fall. On the other hand, there is nothing to show that what is to come will, by the force of things, be but chaos or nothingness, inimical to any nomos. The fiercest confrontation between the old and new forces may as well generate just standards and criteria and forge new dimensions loaded with meaning." Schmitt, LS, 59.

99. See Schmitt, Nomos, 280.

100. Schmitt, Nomos, 354.

101. Schmitt, Nomos, 355.

102. Schmitt, Nomos, 59.

103. Schmitt, Partisan, 23.

104. Schmitt, Partisan, 23.

105. See Schmitt, Partisan, 32.

106. Schmitt, Partisan, 20, 44.

107. See Carl Von Clausewitz, On War, trans. Michael Howard and Peter Paret (Princeton, NJ: Princeton University Press, 1984), 479.

108. Schmitt, Partisan, 47.

109. Schmitt, Partisan, 18.

110. Schmitt, Partisan, 30.

111. Herfried Munkler, Über den Krieg: Stationen der Kriegsgeschichte in Spiegel ihrer theoretischen Reflexion (Weilerswist: Velbrück, 2002), 204, quoted in Gasché, "The Partisan and the Philosopher," 11.

112. Schmitt, Partisan, 38–39.

113. Gasché, "The Partisan and the Philosopher," 28–29.

114. Gasché, "The Partisan and the Philosopher," 25.

115. Gasché, "The Partisan and the Philosopher," 30.

116. For a related discussion of the complex relationship between concepts, polemical terms, and politics see Jacques Derrida, The Politics of Friendship (New York: Verso, 1997), chapter 5.

117. Cf. Schmitt, Partisan, 14: "a spark jumped from Spain to Northern Europe, but up there it did not ignite the same fire that gave the Spanish guerilla war its historical significance." See also Schmitt, Partisan, 48: "Lenin's alliance of philosophy and the partisan unleashed new and explosive forces." See also Schmitt, Partisan, 40: "the spark of national sentiment contaminated the troops."

118. See Schmitt, *Nomos*, 50, fn. 1.

119. Compare the Venician "mythological consecration to a power and a wealth that had been surging from the seas." Schmitt, *LS*, 9.

120. Schmitt, *RC*, 27.

121. Cf. Schmitt, *Partisan*, 41; Schmitt, *Theorie des Partisanen* (Berlin: Duncker and Humblot, 2002), 49.

122. Gasché, "The Partisan and the Philosopher," 25–26, quoting Schmitt, "Clausewitz als politischer Denker: Bemerkungen und Hinweise," *Der Staat* 6.4 (1967).

123. Schmitt, *Partisan*, 14.

124. Schmitt, *Partisan*, 14–15.

125. Schmitt, *Partisan*, 20.

126. Schmitt, *Partisan*, 69–70.

127. Schmitt, *Partisan*, 44.

128. Schmitt, *Partisan*, 78; Schmitt, *Theorie des Partisanen*, 96.

129. Schmitt, *Nomos*, 50, fn. 1.

130. Compare Seneca's words and sentiments of a spherical earth, which "goaded" Columbus. Schmitt, *LS*, 32. See also 45: "Calvinism was the new militant religion, perfectly adapted to the elemental thrust seawards."

131. Schmitt, *LS*, 17. Schmitt also links the British creation of global free trade to the Industrial Revolution. Cf. Schmitt, *LS*, 52–53.

132. Schmitt, *LS*, 18.

133. See Schmitt, *LS*, 21.

134. Schmitt, *Nomos*, 294.

135. See Schmitt, *LS*, 322; Schmitt, *Partisan*, 77.

136. Schmitt, *Partisan*, 77.

137. Schmitt, *Partisan*, 59. Or, in a now familiar metaphorical vein, "all these aspects of the contemporary partisan appear to flow into the technological-industrial aspect that dominates everything." Schmitt, *Partisan*, 64.

138. Cf. Schmitt, *Partisan*, 24–25: "Thus, motorization leads to the partisan losing his telluric character, and he ends up becoming a gear in the mastodontic machine that operates politically on a global level."

139. Schmitt, *Partisan*, 65–66. A similar tone sounds in Schmitt's description of the Whaler and Pirate as outmoded heroic actors in *Land and Sea*.

140. Schmitt, *LS*, 5.

141. Schmitt, "Clausewitz als politischer Denker: Bemerkungen und Hinweise," *Der Staat* 6.4 (1967): 500. Quoted in Gasché, "The Partisan and the Philosopher," 27.

142. Bendersky, "Carl Schmitt at Nuremberg," 128–29. Compare Schmitt, *Nomos*, 125: "But no thought is safe from reinterpretations." Bendersky essentially acquits Schmitt in his commentary on the trial. Cf. "Schmitt at Nuremberg," 91.

~

Carl Schmitt and the Intensification of Politics

Before nations stagger into a total war once more, one must raise the question whether a total enmity truly exists. . . . War and enmity belong to the history of nations. But the worst misfortune only occurs wherever the enmity is generated by the war itself as in the 1914–1918 war, and not as it would be right and sensible, namely that an older, unswayed enmity, true and total to the Day of Judgment, should lead to a total war.—Carl Schmitt

Attempts to apply Schmitt's midcentury critique of international politics to contemporary conflicts no doubt run the risk of conflation. However, current deployment of terms like democracy, sovereignty, and law show such risk to be the very atmosphere of politics. Schmitt was an eloquent critic of migrating political concepts, having witnessed anarchist myths adapted to serve nationalism, liberal neutrality to mask corporate domination, and global pacifism to justify total war. He was also engaged in polemical struggles over the significance of his own concepts. Finally, despite significant transformations, both the institutions and the rhetoric surrounding current forms of global governance exhibit many of the qualities that provoked Schmitt's critique in the 1940s. Universal norms are asserted and global organizations proliferate, but neither a global sovereign nor a global civil society has materialized (though some claim to see the outlines of both on the horizon).[1] Multivalent transgressions of sovereign space and assertions of territorial identity proceed apace. Relations between order and location, friend and enemy, soldier and civilian are confounded. Under these conditions, as Schmitt saw, international norms easily become free-floating sources of legitimacy, crossing but hardly dissolving national lines, alternately circumvented and instrumentalized by powerful interests or hegemons. In response, global liberalism is challenged by left- and right-wing nationalists, as well as radical groups who come to power outside regular channels, organizing their own economic networks, propaganda, and violence. A war on the latter, indeed a war on unconventional war as such (the "War on Terror") has been declared. The expansion of executive emergency powers in its name has been justified using some of the same arguments Schmitt once put forward. The ensuing logic of terror and counterterror has borne out some of Schmitt's worst fears about discriminatory warfare. A plurality of local conflicts bleeds into global polarizations. But what other means might be found for bracketing political conflicts among asymmetrical antagonists?

It is not my aim in this chapter to sort out the complex sources of contemporary political conflicts, much less to propose solutions. Instead, I first highlight recent attempts to apply Schmitt's terms to these conflicts and then offer some initial speculations regarding other relevant insights we might derive, especially from his later works. These works describe the unraveling of sovereign territory by global confluences of commerce, law, technology, and media without falling prey to an image of homogeneous world order. As they show, not only the territorial integrity of the nation-state, but political distinctions more generally depend upon relatively stable relationships among domestic and transnational institutions, cultures, and economies. They emerge from a dynamic combination of traditions and enactments, including norms and decisions but also habits, affections, rhetoric, and images. As these elements shift and blend along with global flows of commerce, labor, war, and media, political distinctions do not disappear, but instead begin to circulate, traversing both territories and genres, combining ethnic, sexual, and aesthetic differences. Intensities are exchanged among diverse antagonisms and new political conflicts come up like mushrooms, "from every domain." As I have argued, Schmitt's work is instructive as both an analytical description and a discursive enactment of these dynamics. It therefore offers us more than a critique of liberal neutrality or a precedent for authoritarian reaction. It also provides insight into the complex means by which contemporary antagonisms become absolute, or might be prevented from becoming so.

Liberal Uses of Schmitt

Schmitt's arguments echo in a variety of contemporary approaches to the new *nomos*, such as Samuel Huntington's proposals for a balance among internally homogeneous *Grossräume*, or "civilizations."[2] Until recently, however, attention has been focused mainly on his critique of liberalism and the neutral state. On the left, this critique has been leveled against a neoliberal world order predicated on the globalization of free trade and human rights, that is, precisely the moral and economic sublimations of political conflict Schmitt lamented.[3] In this vein, Chantal Mouffe and Slavoj Zizek read ethnic nationalism and illiberal religious movements (beginning with those of the former Yugoslavia) as a kind of return of the repressed, not so much the antithesis as a necessary symptom of liberal universalism. Global liberalism, they argue, is not only a fictional screen for U.S. hegemony, but also a vehicle for economic and cultural corrosions that unleash political intensities and contribute to their violent expression.[4] As we have seen, Schmitt also applied his critique of liberalism at the international level, making similar arguments in *The Nomos of the Earth* concerning the economic and cultural erosion of territorial substance within legally sanctified borders on the part of the League of Nations and the United States. In this light, the indirect control exerted through IMF and World Bank institutions over weak states can be seen as a kind of Paris Peace exercised by coalitions of major economic powers, once again in concert with private finance. The concurrent rise of radical, antiliberal parties and regimes invites other comparisons. In Latin America—long subject to U.S. interventions and neoliberal structural adjustments—the turn against liberalism has produced a series of socialist victories, and an enabling act giving the decrees of President Hugo Chavez of Venezuela the power of law. As Vice President Jorge Rodriguez explains, "We want to impose the dictatorship of a true democracy."[5]

While they share a common enemy, Zizek and Mouffe take different positions regarding Schmitt's significance for alternative programs. Zizek embraces a turn to party politics on the Left, though not one restricted to a class or national agenda, siding with Lenin against both liberal and "multicultural" pluralism.[6] As he sees it, Schmitt provides a useful diagnosis of liberal depoliticization, but then ultimately disavows politics—understood as a struggle for symbolic legitimacy or "universalization" that can never be definitively achieved—by reducing it to the extreme form of an extra-discursive opposition.[7] Mouffe instead takes up Schmitt's arguments in the name of what she calls "radical" democratic pluralism. Against a depoliticized liberal order and its illiberal opponents—whom she brands "fundamentalists"—she proposes what amounts to a political liberalism grounded in a substantial ethos (and a specifically European territory) that, ironically enough, excludes cultures and groups unfriendly to an antiessentialist politics, a move that places her in curious proximity with Huntington.[8]

With Schmitt, Mouffe affirms a basic tension between liberal and democratic principles. However, she claims this tension can take a positive form, whereby the friend/enemy antithesis is internalized, and thus ameliorated, as a "friend/adversary" distinction that does not frame difference as an existential threat. Still, a more radical negation is reserved for those who cannot be incorporated as adversaries. As she frankly acknowledges, "The category of the 'enemy' does not disappear but is displaced; it remains pertinent with respect to those who do not accept the democratic 'rules of the game' and who thereby exclude themselves from the political community."[9] Mouffe thus introduces a distinction between kinds, or levels of antagonism, much as Schmitt distinguished bracketed struggles of European opponents from unbounded war with those "beyond the line" in *The Nomos of the Earth*. At issue is the distinction not between friends, but adversaries and enemies.

Mouffe distinguishes herself from Schmitt by misconstruing his arguments regarding the relationship between "concrete" and "constituent" political identity. For Schmitt, she claims, the identity of the people must "be a concrete unity, already given and therefore stable. . . . Because of that, his distinction between 'us' and 'them' is not really politically constructed; it is merely a recognition of already-existing borders."[10] His arguments are therefore "ultimately contradictory." Schmitt creates a "false dilemma," she argues, when he affirms the constituent character of identity and then "requires expelling every division and antagonism outside the demos."[11] As Schmitt makes quite clear, however, political identification is indeed constitutive, and borders are the result of complex and ongoing territorial appropriations. As we saw in chapter 2, the unity of various classes and groupings under the sign of liberal democracy began with a polemical opposition to a common enemy, namely Monarchism.

Mouffe embraces the polemical character of democratic consensus with little reservation. For her, "agreement" on democratic institutions rests not on deliberative norms (which might somehow be universalized), but a loose set of "language games" or an "ensemble of practices . . . [that] make possible the creation of democratic citizens."[12] Furthermore, the unity of these practices requires an opposition to forms of life at odds with democratic values and institutions.

> The real task, in my view, is to foster allegiance to our democratic institutions, and the best way to do this is . . . by creating strong forms of identification with them. This should be done by developing and multiplying in as many social relations as possible the discourses, the practices, the "language games"

that produce democratic "subject positions". The objective is to establish a hegemony of democratic values and practices.[13]

Through this concentration of identification "in as many social relations as possible," the pragmatic "rules of the game" are infused with a hegemonic unity. As a result, the identity of the whole exceeds the particulars that compose it. Mouffe indicates the abstract character of this identity when she attempts to distinguish the enemy proper from a mere "adversary," meaning those with whom we can resolve conflicts within a liberal order and those who remain outside and can only be fought. An adversary is a "legitimate enemy," one "with whom we have some common ground . . . shared adhesion to the ethico-political principles of liberal democracy: liberty and equality."[14] By "adhesion," Mouffe means the "crucial role played by passions and affects in securing allegiance to democratic values."[15] Democratic "values and practices" thus become a kind of *complexio oppositorum*, an emotionally laden set of terms capable of diverse appropriations. All that is left is to distinguish enemies from adversaries. What makes someone an enemy of liberal democracy, and who will decide?

Permanent Danger and Emergency Rule

In the context of a global military mobilization against an enemy publicly defined by their ostensible hatred of liberalism and democracy, Mouffe's proposals have a different resonance.[16] In a perverse way—and certainly at odds with her ostensible commitment to antiessentialism—one could say they have been fulfilled, inasmuch as liberal-democratic hegemony has transcended formal norms and procedures and admitted its antagonistic, or "political" basis, a development culminating in the United States' "War on Terror." With this turn, Schmitt has appeared in another guise. At issue is no longer the sublimation of politics, but its authoritarian concentration, and Schmitt becomes more a dangerous precedent than an instructive critic, linking the permanent danger of an incipient enemy to unlimited executive discretion on the part of the regime that combats it. Along these lines, a variety of authors including Giorgio Agamben, William Scheuerman, Michael Hardt, and Antonio Negri claim that sovereignty now operates in a permanent state of exception, or continuous emergency rule.[17]

Scheuerman's study links contemporary accounts of "social acceleration" with Schmitt's postwar analysis of emergency jurisprudence, outlining a variety of institutional and legal innovations that facilitate a shift of power from legislative to executive and administrative agencies. As he shows, in their attempts to keep up with social acceleration, governments have subordinated constitutional norms and parliamentary legislation in favor of delegated administrative decision-making in congressional committees, nonbinding arbitration, executive agreements, and corporate self-regulation. As we have seen, Schmitt leveraged a similar critique of parliamentary legislation in *Legality and Legitimacy* to bolster his claims for the relative democratic legitimacy of executive decisions. Scheuerman finds another precedent for this transfer of power, linking it more directly to the problem of speed, in Schmitt's 1950 analysis of "motorized lawmaking." The acceleration of social change, he argues, has long favored a general shift of power to the executive branch, classically understood as the "energetic" center of government in times of crisis. However, as was the case when Schmitt wrote, the vague statutes and independent agencies that replace deliberative, participatory legislation are often themselves instrumentalized by other forces, especially organized economic interests.[18] The high-speed executive is therefore itself as much a "myth" as a reality.[19]

Schmitt, certainly, would have criticized the administrative dissemination of decision-making Scheuerman describes. As he argued in *The Nomos of the Earth*, a combination of free trade and *ad hoc* agreements is not likely to create a unity of normative order and spatial orientation. However, contemporary globalization may have transformed the nature of rule in ways that Schmitt failed to fully appreciate. As Hardt, Negri, and Agamben argue, the rule of law over a stable territorial order may no longer be the *modus operandi* of sovereign power. Instead, they discern a mode of global sovereignty that thrives on cultural and territorial hybridity.[20] Gilles Deleuze and Felix Guattari's term "deterritorialization" is therefore apt, inasmuch as, like *nomos*, it applies not only to spatial boundaries but to the distribution and allocation of social and cultural categories.[21] Furthermore, they argue that rather than a singular site of decision, contemporary sovereignty takes the form of decentralized managerial or police powers on the part of various political, economic, and nongovernmental authorities.

These descriptions of continuous emergency power draw on earlier studies by Paul Virilio, Deleuze, and Guattari. In *Speed and Politics* (1986), Virilio traces the spatial dislocations of our age to the evolution of military technologies that facilitated an exponential increase in the flow of information, populations, and violence around the globe.[22] Like Schmitt, Virilio describes this erasure of territoriality as an extension of the spatial logic of the seas. However, he argues the elemental atmosphere of human activity has become neither air nor fire, but time. The sovereign guarantee of spatial order has been replaced by the temporal management of various global flows, or what Virilio calls "logistics." Under conditions of rapid socio-economic and cultural change, war also ceases to be a discrete event and becomes a potentially continuous engagement. His early diagnosis remains among the most incisive: "The ancient inter city duel, war between nations, the permanent conflict between naval empires and continental powers have all suddenly disappeared, giving way to an unheard-of opposition: the juxtaposition of every locality, all matter. . . . In the future the earth will have but one interface."[23]

As Hardt and Negri see it, this future has arrived. Moreover, they subsume the plurality of agencies and institutions associated with logistics, in what they describe as a *de facto* global sovereign, or "Empire." As they describe it, Empire is a unified "capitalist sovereignty" that includes not only diverse forms of power but also the discourses and ideologies that legitimate them, allocating not only material value but social and cultural identities.[24] Writing in 1987, Piccone and Ulmen had already come to a similar view.

> Even Schmitt's own modification of the concept of "economic imperialism" with the "tyranny of values" is itself obsolete. The tyranny is gone. Today the mechanism of imperialism is mediated throughout by a culture industry which guarantees socio-economic hegemony by rendering the rest of the world subliminally dependent on what advanced industrial societies can profitably produce and distribute. No longer in need of being imposed from above, because it is now demanded from below, cultural imperialism new enjoys a legitimacy undreamt by earlier forms of imperialism.[25]

To some extent, these authors confuse the two kinds of total state Schmitt described, mistaking "total through weakness" for "total through strength."[26] One might say such confusion is appropriate, as it is difficult to tell when the state is a tyrant, an instrument, or both. However, Hardt and Negri ultimately subsume these alternatives by conflating state, military, nongovernmental and corporate power, describing them as components of a single "network." Of course, they insist Empire is itself only a reaction to the ineradicable forces of creative struggles. Further, they unite these struggles under the common sign of a global revolutionary subject, the Multitude. Moreover, they depict the confrontation between these world-historical enemies as approaching its ultimate conclusion. Like the "irrational" variants of Marxism Schmitt described, their discourse comprises a powerful myth, organizing diverse grievances around the vague and powerful image of an enemy whose overthrow is historically inevitable, and imminent.[27]

Enmities among Us: Terror and the Partisan

If we put such myths aside, the global interface Virilio describes would seem less susceptible to Manichean polarities. Rather than a single opposition, the "juxtaposition of every locality" (or every "face") results in a volatile blend of differences, giving rise to a plurality of mutable conflicts. The supposed tools of Empire, including the "culture industry" look less like the arms of a global hegemon than a disjointed array of weapons, media technologies, emotionally charged scripts, and images that are appropriated by state and nonstate actors for many purposes. Thus, we see neither the sublimation of conflict nor the concentration of sovereign power, but mobile, eruptive political struggles. As I have argued, Schmitt's work traces a similar development along parallel trajectories from the Catholic ethos of belief to the pathos of identification described in *The Concept of the Political* and from a stable *nomos* to deterritorialized partisan groupings. At the intersection of volatile transnational forces, violent political confrontations can arise from sundry class, religious, and aesthetic antagonisms, the intensities of which are modified by events near and far. The points at which new hostilities intensify and politicize, moreover, do not fall along a clear line of development. Rather, distant events or new ideas can suddenly organize dispersed energies, resulting in dramatic eruptions of violence, or as Schmitt puts it, an "ambiguous designation can suddenly become profoundly political."[28] Because these transformations do not follow from the primordial composition of local groupings, Arjun Appadurai describes the emergence of ethnic violence as an "implosion" of local and global forces rather than an explosion of inherent tendencies.[29] This possibility is also captured, albeit more crassly, by Benjamin Barber's phrase (not to be confused with his book's bombastic title), "Jihad *via* McWorld."[30]

On the side of sovereignty, formal hostilities between symmetrical powers have been supplanted not by a comprehensive form of global control, but by ongoing, fragmented, or "limited" warfare, perhaps better termed by Sylvere Lotringer "State terrorism."[31] In *A Thousand Plateaus*, Deleuze and Guattari display similar prescience. The new war machine, they write, has "set its sights on a new type of enemy, no longer another State, or even another regime, but the 'unspecified enemy.'"[32] In light of recent developments, these formulations gain an air of clairvoyance. As recent commentaries from across the political spectrum show, it is all too easy to draw parallels between Schmitt's ideas and the polemical definition of enemies of liberal democracy in the Bush administration's strategy and rhetoric surrounding the "war on terror."[33] This enemy today is notoriously vague, characterized precisely by a lack of territorial or legal integrity. In the name of a global war against it, the United States has made substantial progress toward a unilateral order only to reveal the limits of such a project (an embarrassing symptom being the enduring failure of intelligence agencies to uncover Osama bin Laden, still at large as of this writing, over six years after 9/11). On the whole, the occasional, violent assertion of universal norms has taken precedence over attempts to define them in concrete terms. Waged against criminalized and stateless groups ("unlawful enemy combatants"), or "criminal" states, the war on terror proceeds by extrajudicial decrees, secret detention centers, administrative delegations, constitutional evasions, and a general preference for the *Arcanum* over open discussion.

Despite conceptual and territorial complexities, clearly, simplifying myths cannot so easily be set aside. The aforementioned bombast of Barber's 1995 title, *Jihad vs. McWorld*, now seems prescient. As Schmitt noted, philosophical "consecrations" of partisan struggles, combined with new technologies of war and communication, can channel them into global ideological oppositions. In the neoconservative rhetoric of the George W. Bush administration, the war on terror is a global struggle against "evil," for God, humanity, and justice. While initially framed as a "crusade" (inviting comparisons to Schmitt's "right and sensible" theological confrontation), it subsequently became a war for freedom, democracy, order, human rights, and civilization, all under the auspices of a "moral law that stands above men and nations."[34] In Bush's 2003 speech to the United Nations assembly, all nations are called to join this battle, whose special agents include both the United Nations and the United States.

> Events during the past two years have set before us the clearest of divides: between those who seek order, and those who spread chaos; between those who work for peaceful change, and those who adopt the methods of gangsters; between those who honor the rights of man, and those who deliberately take the lives of men and women and children without mercy or shame. Between these alternatives there is no neutral ground. All governments that support terror are complicit in a war against civilization. . . . And all nations that fight terror, as if the lives of their own people depend on it, will earn the favorable judgment of history. . . . The founding documents of the United Nations and the founding documents of America stand in the same tradition. Both assert that human beings should never be reduced to objects of power or commerce, because their dignity is inherent. Both require—both recognize a moral law that stands above men and nations, which must be defended and enforced by men and nations.[35]

We find in this speech a multifaceted de-humanization of the enemy. The terrorist is denied humanity, morality, religion, and civilization. Looking at Bush's second inaugural speech, we find a similar set of incantations.[36] The march of freedom is historically inevitable (not running on "wheels of inevitability," but still displaying a "visible direction"), divinely ordained, continuous, and institutionally flexible.[37] Broadly speaking, Bush's speeches replicate the combination of enmities with a prophetic anticipation of a final struggle that Schmitt found effective in messianic Marxism. Under the sign of terror, a plurality of local struggles, including that over a Palestinian state, have been conflated. However, justifications for the war more clearly resemble the medieval language of just war previously overcome by the *Jus Publicum Europaeum*. Moreover, the role of United States as the final arbiter had already been asserted in the doctrine of "preemption," which places the United States, and the executive branch in particular, in the position to decide not only when and how to wage war, but also to prevent terror.[38]

As in the wars Schmitt described, the moral criminalization of the terrorist enemy has also combined with his technological de-humanization by remote warfare. In the war on terror, death is made abstract by long-range missiles, satellite surveillance, and remotely piloted aircraft.[39] Indeed, the electronic simulation of military space has been made an explicit policy aim in "informational" or "net-centric" warfare, based on a real time electronic mapping of the battlefield, or even the entire earth (an aspiration driving the construction of a "Global Information Grid" or GIG).[40] These technologies have not so much disconnected us from violence as they have dislocated the context of that violence, as digital media carry death and torture back home across satellites and the Internet for media spectacles and private consumption. Moreover, the attempt to impose unilateral force and perspective, while highly destructive, has failed to effectively distinguish combatants from civilians or produce a stable ground for the rule of law. In this light, the popularity of messianic Christianity in contemporary America can be seen less as a cause than a consolation for U.S. foreign policy.[41] Without the creation of a new *nomos*, attending to the production and allocation of goods and positions, only a total isolation or destruction of the groupings capable of political alignment (the civilian "infrastructure" out of which the insurgency arises) can halt partisan hostilities. Indeed, a recent editorial anticipates, and implicitly recommends, just that. Edward Wong quotes Sheik Muhammad Bakr Khamis al-Suhail, an ostensible supporter of the American push for democracy in Iraq: "We need strong rulers or dictators like Franco, Hitler, even Mubarak. We need a strong dictator, and a fair one at the same time, to kill all extremists, Sunni and Shiite."[42] Wong explains, "It is for people like him that the Americans have fought this war. But the solution he proposes is not one the Americans would easily embrace."[43] Thus, as Schmitt argued, the technological deterritorialization of air war results in an absolute violence that demands a moral absolutism justifying a scorched earth. Despite Donald Rumsfeld's proclamations concerning the radical transformation of the battlefield by new technologies, then, much remains the same. From the U.S. carpet-bombing of Vietnam and the Soviet devastation of Afghanistan to "shock and awe" in the Iraq desert and Israel's summer 2006 bombing of Lebanon, the use of air campaigns to impose a stable order on the land below has been at once a spectacular failure and a failed spectacle. At the same time, these spectacles may serve another purpose, coercing domestic moral support, however ephemeral, for a wartime administration.

It would hardly have surprised Schmitt to find embargoes, torture, and mass killing proceeding in the name of a vague, overarching global humanism. In his later works, we have seen, Schmitt was very much concerned with the spread of war beyond territorial, ethical, and legal boundaries. He would no doubt have been alarmed to find "just war" transcending the defensive function articulated in the Monroe Doctrine to become a preemptive right of intervention (on the part of the United States, anyway).[44] One catches a reflection of his sentiments in the words of Walter Laqueur, who writes, "there can be no final victor in the fight against terrorism [a point Bush momentarily acknowledged], for terrorism (rather than full-scale war) is the contemporary manifestation of conflict, and conflict will not disappear from the earth."[45] As Schmitt discovered, much too late, the *Katechon* and the *Archeront* can trade places.[46] Under the sign of a defensive struggle for normalcy, the sovereign identification of enemies can give way to an occasional justification for indefinite war. This time, bin Laden plays the inverted Dulcinea, inspiring a quixotic military adventure against his many shadows.

Moving Centers:
Leadership, Democracy, and Gravity

The new West claimed to be the true West, the true Occident, the true Europe. . . . International law ceased to have its center of gravity in old Europe. The center of civilization shifted further west, to America. —Carl Schmitt

Now, you're thinking of Europe as Germany and France. I don't. I think that's old Europe. If you look at the entire NATO Europe today, the center of gravity is shifting to the east.—Donald Rumsfeld

As noted earlier, the later Schmitt's alarm at the prospect of unbounded hostilities can appear more or less ironic, depending how one explains earlier shifts in his perspective. Before he became so concerned with asymmetrical war, after all, Schmitt wrote precisely to justify the extension of emergency powers, both for domestic control and international expansion. To this end, he eventually grounded supralegal presidential authority in the vague "confidence" (*Vertrauen*) of a democratic public, a source of legitimacy linked tenuously, at best, to a substantial culture or a concrete set of laws and institutions. Recently, we have seen executive discretion framed in a similar manner by one of the architects of the Iraq War, the former Secretary of Defense Donald Rumsfeld. In an interview following the 2001 attacks on the World Trade Center, Rumsfeld draws an analogy between the matrix of authority, democracy, and enemies in the war on terror and that of the Cold War.

> In country after country, leaders kind of rose to the top and persuaded and informed the American people so that they gained the support necessary to make investments, in a time of peace, to make investments that would enable us to defend, if necessary—but preferably deter—against a very serious, persistent, expansionist, powerful threat that was not visible, that wasn't there every minute, that people wanted to debate against as to whether it even existed, and the American people had the staying power. And they will this time. My hope is that they'll have it because of the fact that the need is there and that democratic people, free people, have a pretty good center of gravity. The other way they'll have it is if we're punctuated periodically with additional terrorist attacks that remind us that we do have an obligation to ourselves and our system and our friends and allies around the world to behave responsibly.[47]

During the Cold War, the integrity of liberal democracy was consolidated in opposition to Communism and the Soviet military threat. As Rumsfeld emphasizes, this threat was largely abstract, or "invisible." Nonetheless, American people had the "staying power," sustained by their democratic "center of gravity." The center of gravity signifies a base of support for sovereign decisions that exceeds rational calculation. Described as gravity, this support is granted an aura of determinate force and direction. However, as Rumsfeld allows, a center of gravity can be modified by contributing actions, or "jolts," including the persuasive power of individual leaders and occasional attacks. Indeed, he conflates the latter two, however unwittingly. On one hand, authority is sustained not only by violence but persuasion. On the other hand, persuasion is not only as much a matter of explanation but also of force. Furthermore, violence itself has a discursive function. The exception, the break in the otherwise endless flow of discussion is, in his terms, "periodic;" it is not the end of argument, but a "punctuation" that modulates it.

When pressed on the popular legitimacy of various administrative policies, Rumsfeld reiterates his confidence in the American "center of gravity." In numerous speeches and interviews, he appeals to a surplus of popular support over and above specific expectations or beliefs that sustains authority. In perhaps his most infamous speech, Rumsfeld uses the phrase in conjunction with his distinction between "old" and "new" Europe, describing a shifting "center of gravity" from France and Germany to the eastern reaches of NATO.

> I was ambassador to NATO, and I—when we would go in and make a proposal, there wouldn't be unanimity. There wouldn't even be understanding. And we'd have to be persuasive. We'd have to show reasons. We'd have to—have to give rationales. We'd have to show facts. And, by golly, I found that Europe on any major issue is given—if there's leadership and if you're right, and if your facts are persuasive, Europe responds. And they always have. Now, you're thinking of Europe as Germany and France. I don't. I think that's old Europe. If you look at the entire NATO Europe today, the center of gravity is shifting to the east. . . . Now, you cite public opinion polls. Fair enough. Political leaders have to interest themselves in where the public is, and talk to them, and think about that, and then—and provide leadership to them. . . . And that's—that's what political leaders are supposed to do, is to lead.[48]

As Rousseau argued, leaders need to persuade, creating a blend of facts and reasons that resonates with a given public. In Rumsfeld's speech, the shift in gravity from old to new Europe concerns the relative responsiveness of the latter to persuasive leadership, unlike those Western European democracies more sensitive to swings in popular opinion (as indicated by his dismissive reference to polls). Like the mobilizing myth of the bourgeois enemy Schmitt described in The Crisis of Parliamentary Democracy, America's war gains support as it moves east, resonating with local ideas and—as others noted at the time—authoritarian traditions.

Like Schmitt's complexio oppositorum, Rumsfeld's "center of gravity" can be found at multiple, related levels, in the psyche of the American people, on the battlefield, and so forth.[49] It involves both a fund of legitimate authority and contributions made to that fund by a combination of force and persuasion, or as Rumsfeld puts it, the cumulative effect of various "pressures" (economic, military, etc.).[50] Rumsfeld's use of the phrase thus displays a nuanced (albeit intuitive) conception of legitimate power and its exercise, recognizing both the relative fungibility of affections and hostilities that exceeds particular objects (allowing them to contribute "gravity" to collective identity and enmity) and the plurality of positive sources from which they are drawn. In Rumsfeld's discourse, as in Schmitt's, identification, enmity, and action take shape out of a conflation of diverse elements that contributes to a generalized intensity or pressure. Once combined, each element is infused with the intensities of the others with which it resonates. (Consider the rhetorical conflation of the liberal media; European, especially French, traitors or ingrates; foreign enemies; and domestic critics in the rhetoric of the Republican Party at the time.) Thus, the American democratic center of gravity both facilitates and feeds on a campaign against sundry enemies whose coherence is assured precisely by their lack of specificity.

The terrorist enemy so described conforms to Sorel's definition of a political myth. As Schmitt noted, the strength of such a myth corresponds to that of the sentiments evoked by the image of the enemy. Just as Italian fascism's Mongolian Bolshevism was a more compelling threat than the decadent bourgeois, Osama bin Laden produces a greater charge than Ken Lay (a passing symbol of corporate corruption).[51] As David Brooks succinctly puts it (taking John Kerry to task for insufficiently focused hostility toward the bin Laden during his 2004 presidential campaign), "We are revealed by what we hate."[52] Brooks thus adopts a primordialist thesis of the individual psyche, placing political hatred at the core of personal identity. "Kerry hasn't revealed whatever it is that lies inside."[53] However, as Schmitt's analysis of political antagonisms suggests, we are not so much revealed as constituted by the accumulation and channeling of various enmities and affections. Like that of the ethnic groups Appadurai describes, our hate is implosive. Appadurai draws on the work of Stanley Tambiah, who describes the emergence of ethnic violence as a function of "transvaluation and focalization," terms that clearly echo the basic psychic operations of condensation and displacement described by Freud and Lacan. He explains, "focalization progressively denudes local incidents and disputes of their contextual particulars, and transvaluation distorts, abstracts, and aggregates those incidents into larger collective issues of national or ethnic interest."[54] As we saw in Schmitt's description of the Catholic *complexio oppositorum*, these operations apply not only to the psyche, but also to discursive and iconographic practices (Tambiah also emphasizes the role of music) that evoke and combine a plurality of hatreds and affections. Such an operation was accomplished with particular economy by the slogan "support the troops," widely adopted and much criticized during the first years of the Iraq War. In its abstraction, the phrase acts as a repudiation of instrumentality—goals are not supported, but militarization itself—of criticism, and of individuation. "Support" becomes an act without a subject or an aim. At the same time, it draws on rich cultural polarities, evoking all who might in one way or another refuse this support. Any number of enemies of the troops could be conflated, from antiwar activists to Donald Rumsfeld himself, who was taken to task for the insufficient provision of material support, especially protective armor, for soldiers on the ground in Iraq.

It is no accident that Rumsfeld's formulations of the relationship between leaders and the population resemble those of Clausewitz, who coined the phrase "center of gravity," and remains a key source for war planners in the Pentagon. Clausewitz, Schmitt tells us, "assigned to the people only the 'blind natural instinct' of hatred and hostility, to the commander-in-chief and his army 'courage and talent.'"[55] Schmitt, we have seen, conceived a similar relationship between the executive and the demos.[56] Gravity, for Rumsfeld, indicates the uncritical force of popular affections that allows for flexible decision-making on the part of leaders. Much as Schmitt refigured the affective receptivity of the romantic (whom he described precisely as lacking a "center of gravity" in *Political Romanticism*) in a positive direction when describing presidential popularity in *Legality and Legitimacy*, Rumsfeld frames receptiveness to leadership and persuasion as a substantial form of democratic agency. In short, gravity is his *Vertrauen*. For Clausewitz, however, the center of gravity was not a source of power or agency, but rather, as Antulio Echevarria of the U.S. Army War College argues, a focal point of convergent forces. "In modern elementary physics, which was about the state of the mechanical sciences in Clausewitz's day, a CoG represents the point where the forces of gravity converge within an object. Striking at the CoG with enough force will usually cause the object to lose its balance, or equilibrium, and fall. A CoG is, therefore, *not* a source of strength, but a factor of Balance."[57] Echevarria offers the following definition: "Centers of Gravity are *focal points* that serve to hold a combatant's entire system or structure together and that draw power from a variety of sources and provide it with purpose and direction."[58] The center, one might say, is a *coincidentia* of forces rather than a *complexio* that binds them. If we apply this perspective to the center of gravity Rumsfeld attributes to the American public, confidence in leaders or their foreign policy appears less a source of guidance than a convergence of forces and their manipulation.

Ultimately, in the face of military failures, absent sufficient reminders (the color-coded terror alert system is no substitute for violent attacks) and perhaps—one can hope—aided by an antiauthoritarian countermemory, the American center of gravity shifted, and Rumsfeld was forced to resign from his position in 2006. His "light footprint" response to occasional conflicts—rather than a traditional ground occupation—has been pejoratively redescribed by

Senator John McCain as a "whack-a-mole" approach that fails to establish a secure territorial situation.[59] Of course, others had criticized the war along these lines from the outset. While relatively few—at least in the popular media of the United States—suppose the war on terror is merely a pretext for indefinite military imperialism, many have warned that the identification and pursuit of so-called terrorists may itself multiply the enemies it ostensibly aims to destroy, however unwittingly. Thus, in response to neo realist scholars' invocations of just war, traditional realists have sought from the beginning to restrict the war to a struggle over discrete interests and objectives. Prominent among them is Zbigniew Brzezinski, former national security advisor to Jimmy Carter and an intellectual heir of Hans Morgenthau (himself one of Schmitt's interlocutors). Brzezinski reproaches the Bush administration for its ideological definition of the terrorist threat, insisting that the enemy be concretely defined as a set of individuals or groups rather than as an "abstraction."[60] He laments the deterritorialization of enmity in the mythological vagaries of the administration's rhetoric.

> It deals with abstractions. It theologizes the challenge. It doesn't point directly at the problem. It talks about a broad phenomenon, terrorism, as the enemy overlooking the fact that terrorism is a technique for killing people. That doesn't tell us who the enemy is. It's as if we said that World War II was not against the Nazis but against blitzkrieg. We need to ask who is the enemy, and the enemies are terrorists. But not in an abstract, theologically defined fashion, people, to quote again our highest spokesmen, "people who hate things, whereas we love things"—literally. Not to mention the fact that of course terrorists hate freedom. I think they do hate. But believe me, I don't think they sit there abstractly hating freedom. They hate some of us. They hate some countries. They hate some particular targets. But it's a lot more concrete than these vague quasi-theological formulations.[61]

In this passage, Brzezinski ironically inverts the prevailing distinction between liberals and terrorists, according to which it is precisely the latter who are driven by vague theological hatred. However, in his earlier study of totalitarianism with Carl Friedrich, Brzezinski emphasizes the continuity of liberal and illiberal regimes along these lines, pointing to their shared mythological rhetoric.

> [Totalitarian regimes] substitute faith for reason, magic exhortation for knowledge and criticism. And yet it must be recognized that there are enough of these same elements in the operations of democratic parties to attest to the relation between them and their perverted descendants, the totalitarian movements.

That is why these movements must be seen and analyzed in their relationship to the democracy they seek to supplant.[62]

In seeking a concrete definition of enemies, Brzezinski suggests we follow the terrorists' lead and focus our hatred on discrete targets. Otherwise, the identification of an Islamic enemy will become self-fulfilling, a preemptive conflation of enmities. "American rhetoric and actions increase the likelihood that the moderates will eventually unite with the jihadists in outraged anger and unite the world of Islam in a head-on collision with America."[63] American military actions are themselves generating a volatile complex. "Nationalism is blending with religious fanaticism into a potent brew of hatreds" resulting in a complementary conflation of American and Israeli policies and outlooks.[64]

Looking forward, Brzezinski goes so far as to anticipate a replication of the global polarization of a reactionary "Holy Alliance" opposed to popular revolutions in the early nineteenth century. His alternative proposition is a "grand alliance" that would incorporate Middle Eastern states by way of "economically beneficial normalization of relations with the West."[65] His emphasis on economic relations, and his provisions for the Israeli-Palestinian conflict, including a demilitarized Palestinian state, would no doubt have caused Schmitt to raise an eyebrow.[66] Nonetheless, his frustration over the mytho-poetical constitution of "objective" enemies echoes Schmitt's. However, he lacks the terms to grasp the combination of vague intensities and specific instantiations at work on both sides of the current conflict. The Bush administration, meanwhile, has refused to countenance these ironies, at least in its public rhetoric. Bush himself has defensively insisted, "You don't create terrorists by defending yourself and fighting back. You defeat the terrorists by fighting back."[67] Just as Israel's targeting of militants does little to address the sources of militancy, and, whether cynically or inadvertently, promotes the drive to martyrdom that further vindicates exceptional security measures, the United States' logic of "fighting terrorists on their soil" ignores (or cynically dissimulates) the constitutive dimension of a definition of enemies.

Conclusions and Qualifications

Because existential oppositions can channel energies from a variety of local conflicts, it is no easy matter to distinguish the telluric from the global partisan. As I have argued, Schmitt's discussions of enmity and identity complicate both realist and idealist/neo-conservative perspectives. They suggest the identification of enemies to the collective cannot be deduced from a set of objective interests or moral principles alone. Nor can the hostility of these enemies be restricted to a specific set of objective targets. On both sides, identity and enmity accumulate, drawing energy from a variety of struggles and positive conditions all of which are transfigured in the resulting combinations. Hostility is conditioned by a plurality of positive factors without being simply derived from any of them. Hence, those thinkers who distinguish a clash of ideas from economic grievances are right to do so, and those who see the two as linked are also correct. We find these arguments side by side in an article by Laqueur subtitled, "The Rules of Law and Warfare Do Not Apply." Laqueur first rejects economic explanations of terrorism, which stems not from clear goals but "free-floating aggression." However, he then suggests this aggression reflects an accumulation of resentments from sexual repression as well as economic and educational marginalization (particularly in second-generation immigrants).[68] Likewise, for Schmitt the political cannot be reduced to the economic, aesthetic, or moral antagonisms from which it draws intensities. Because it is overdetermined, one cannot reduce terror to a discrete cause. However, Schmitt's analysis of particular struggles suggests that while aggressions can float, they are nonetheless conditioned by positive factors that lend both direction and intensity to a given political orientation. Enmity is neither a pure energy nor fixed to discrete objects, but a blend of circulating tendencies that can be catalyzed by diverse environmental factors and that bind with some myths more effectively than others.

A variety of inferences might be drawn from this discussion. As Schmitt argues—and recent history confirms—"latent civil war" can inhabit relatively stable channels of difference and affiliation. We are ceaselessly reminded, lest we become irresponsible, that terrorists can arise anywhere, at any place or time. Yet, for the same reasons, a spark does not always ignite a fire (that issuing from the Spanish Civil War, recall, smoldered until the right conditions arose for later explosions). Just as they can arise suddenly, intense combinations can be dampened at multiple points or stages in their accumulation. Like fascism in Weimar, partisan identifications today operate "at widely varying levels of intensity . . . at one moment, ethnic conflict may appear to eclipse all other factors in the political equation; a few years later, the same cleavage may appear entirely muted."[69] Because constitutive identifications of friends and enemies draw on these circulating intensities, their effects will also vary. As Schmitt wrote, "The Archeron cannot be planned and does not appear every time it is invoked."[70] Likewise the American center of gravity, as Rumsfeld discovered.

We might apply these insights to the emergence of Schmitt's concepts in the midst of unstable political and discursive conditions. As Schmitt argued regarding Sorel's political myth, "bellicose, revolutionary excitement and the expectation of monstrous catastrophes belong to the intensity of life and move history. But the momentum must come from the masses themselves; ideologists and intellectuals cannot create it."[71] The reader may also recall Balakrishnan's description of Schmitt's work as an "explosively unstable combination." Schmitt's work channels powerful currents. At the same time, it can be turned in a number of directions, including against itself. As we have seen, his perspective vacillates between justification and critique, alternately analyzing and promulgating the mythological unity of political collectives, sometimes in the same text.[72] As I have suggested, both analytic and rhetorical dimensions of Schmitt's work are therefore instructive. When closely observed, they illuminate the fraught relationship between theory, rhetoric, and politics in times of crisis, reminding us we remain responsible for the enemies we do not simply choose.

In light of Schmitt's biography, these reflections may seem discouraging. For him, the weakness of norms in the face of contingent material forces motivated a turn to supranormative authority that ended in the worst of disasters. He would later write, "All of this teaches that a normative regulation of the problem of the partisan is juridically impossible."[73] However, as Schmitt's account of *nomos* indicates, the deterritorialization and amplification of partisan warfare can be mitigated by other than "normative" means or the broadly construed powers of an ostensibly commissarial dictator. The fluidity of enmity and the power of myth should not lead us to conclude either that material interests or moral principles are epiphenomena in political conflicts, only that they gather shape and intensity from other sources. Social welfare, immigration policies, media organization, education, police tactics, public architecture, and a variety of other mediating factors may help decide whether a local struggle for resources and recognition is caught up in a global, unlimited war. A "complex of opposites" can be manipulated by those with specific aims and strategies, but it can also be subject to rhetorical challenge and critical reflection. I believe Schmitt's work provides opportunities for both. Despite, or rather because of his personal and theoretical alignments, a study of Schmitt's texts should encourage, not discourage, the formulation of more creative and nuanced responses to political antagonism. As I have argued, his arguments can alert us to the seemingly paradoxical dynamics between substantial and constitutive identifications, including the fact that concrete identifications of enemies can serve the accumulation of surplus authority and contribute to a generalized enmity, potentially magnifying and expanding violent confrontations.

Such identifications, of course, do not invent enemies in an otherwise peaceful world; rather, they contribute to the polarization and intensity of antagonism. The identification of friends and enemies remains a transformative act, but one made precarious by the sources on which it draws and the means by which the struggle against enemies proceeds. Rather than simply identifying enemies, then, we can also work on mitigating and deferring oppositional antagonisms. In particular, diverse sources of enmity need to be considered in concert, including those tactical struggles Schmitt dismissed as beneath political concern. Rather than seeking a convergence of economic, religious, aesthetic, and political commitments, strategies might instead be formulated to enhance their potential for mutual critique. Because of the dynamic character of enmity, enemies will continue to arise from unexpected quarters, and attempts to prevent this will sometimes fail. However, contra Schmitt, there is no "right and sensible" or "unswayed" conflict that must, or should, lead to total war.

This brief discussion is by no means meant to exhaust the legal and political questions raised by the war on terror and its link to the project of democratization, or to untangle the contradictory blend of policies, rhetoric, and stratagems currently in play. In closing, I propose that Schmitt's later works offer us more than a critique of global liberalism, an insistence on irreducible antagonism, or a model for supralegal authority, without therefore providing solutions to any of these problems. Schmitt's writings highlight extranormative dimensions of politics that underpin both sovereign decisions and objective struggles between friends and enemies. Read in the right light, they help us shift our attention instead to diverse avenues from which political antagonism arises and by which it can therefore be amplified, mitigated, or redirected, though never finally eliminated. In his (entirely questionable) depiction of the *Jus Publicum Europaeum*, Schmitt describes a dynamic pluralism reducible neither to positive norms nor concrete borders. A similarly dynamic global pluralism remains a distant, all but unthinkable aspiration. In order to achieve the latter, legal rights need to be combined with passionate attachments and ethical relations that follow the paths of material connections between mobile, shifting collectives. Rather than a guide, Schmitt provides a set of resources and challenges for those who seek agonistic modes of pluralism that can be formulated, first of all, as questions: Who can be just enemies today? Is a bracketed antagonism possible that does not distinguish just enemies from those "beyond the line?" What military, economic, aesthetic, and institutional factors now amplify or mitigate antagonism among given groupings? For those of us on the left, another question must be added that is not derived from Schmitt, namely, how might a bracketing of antagonism be achieved *democratically*? That is, how might the diverse factors shaping collective antagonism themselves become sites of popular reflection and contest, and how can political philosophy contribute to this end?

Notes

1. Claims regarding a global sovereign are discussed below. On the rise of a global civil society, see Manuel Castells, "Global Governance and Global Politics." *Political Science and Politics* 38.1 (2005): 9–16.

2. Cf. Samuel P. Huntington, "The Clash of Civilizations?" *Foreign Affairs* 72 (Summer 1993): 22–49.

3. Cf. Jan-Werner Müller, *A Dangerous Mind*. New Haven, CT: Yale University Press, 2003, 221.

4. Cf. Slavoj Zizek, "Carl Schmitt in the Age of Post-Politics," in *The Challenge of Carl Schmitt*, ed. Chantal Mouffe (New York: Verso, 1999), 35; Chantal Mouffe, *The Return of the Political* (New York: Verso, 1993), 6; Chantal Mouffe, *The Democratic Paradox* (New York: Verso, 2000), 96. See also Zizek, "Multiculturalism, or the Logic of Multinational Capitalism," *New Left Review* (September–October 1997).

5. Cf. "Chávez Gets Power to Rule by Decree." *USA Today*, February 1, 2007, www.usatoday.com/printedition/news/20070201/a_chavez01.art.htm.

6. Cf. Slavoj Zizek, *The Ticklish Subject* (New York: Verso, 1999), 236.

7. Cf. Zizek, "Carl Schmitt in the Age of Post-Politics," 29, 35.

8. Cf. Mouffe, *Paradox*, 127. "Of course such an answer can only be carried out successfully in a European context, and this is why a left-wing project today can only be a European one."

9. Mouffe, *Return*, 4.

10. Mouffe, *Paradox*, 54.

11. Mouffe, *Paradox*, 52–54.

12. Mouffe, *Paradox*, 95.

13. Mouffe, *Return*, 151. See also *Paradox*, 96: "Democratic individuals can only be made possible by multiplying the institutions, the discourses, the forms of life that foster identification with democratic values."

14. Mouffe, *Paradox*, 102.

15. Mouffe, *Paradox*, 95.

16. Admittedly, as Jan-Werner Müller points out, liberalism had already taken a political, militarized form in the Kosovo war. Cf. Müller, *A Dangerous Mind*, 226.

17. Cf. Michael Hardt and Antonio Negri, *Empire* (Cambridge, MA: Harvard University Press, 2000), 18; Giorgio Agamben, *State of Exception*, trans. Kevin Attell (Chicago: University of Chicago Press, 2005), 14; Piccone and Ulmen, "Introduction to Carl Schmitt," *Telos* 72 (Summer 1987): 3–14, 11; McCormick, "Introduction," in *Legaliät und Legitimität*, Carl Schmitt (Munchen: Duncker & Humblot, 1932); Wil-

liam Scheuerman, *Liberal Democracy and the Social Acceleration of Time* (Baltimore, MD: Johns Hopkins University Press, 2004); and my review of the last in *Perspectives on Politics* 3.2 (June 2005): 360–61.

18. Scheuerman, *Acceleration*, 216. See also Ingeborg Maus, "The 1933 Break."

19. Scheuerman, *Acceleration*, 192–93.

20. See "Sovereignty, Multitudes, Absolute Democracy: A Discussion between Michael Hardt and Thomas Dumm about Hardt and Negri's Empire." *Theory and Event* 4.3, par. 23. Cf. Agamben, *State of Exception*, 8.

21. Cf. Gilles Deleuze and Felix Guattari, *A Thousand Plateaus* (Minneapolis: University of Minnesota Press, 1987).

22. Cf. Paul Virilio, *Speed and Politics*, trans. Mark Polizzotti (New York: Semiotext(e), 1986).

23. Virilio, *Speed and Politics*, 136.

24. Cf. Hardt and Negri, *Empire*, 385.

25. Piccone and Ulmen, "Introduction to Carl Schmitt," 10.

26. Cf. Jean-Francois Kervégan, "Carl Schmitt and 'World Unity,'" in *The Challenge of Carl Schmitt*, ed. Chantal Mouffe (New York: Verso, 1999), 35.

27. I explore these parallels at greater length in "The Myth of the Multitude," *The Empire's New Clothes* (New York: Routledge, 2003).

28. Carl Schmitt, *Theory of the Partisan*, trans. G. L. Ulmen, *Telos* 127 (Spring 2004): 11–78.

29. Arjun Appadurai, *Modernity at Large* (Minneapolis: University of Minnesota Press, 1996), 149.

30. Cf. Benjamin Barber, *Jihad vs. McWorld* (New York: Times Books, 1995), chapter 10.

31. Paul Virilio and Sylvere Lotringer, *Pure War* (New York: Semiotext(e), 1983), 36.

32. Deleuze and Guattari, *A Thousand Plateaus*, 422.

33. Cf. Jan-Werner Müller, *A Dangerous Mind*, 226–29. For more journalistic treatments, see Alan Wolfe, "A Fascist Philosopher Helps Us Understand Contemporary Politics," *The Chronicle Review* 50.30 (2004): B16; Barbara Boyd, "Dick Cheney's Éminence Grise: A Profile of Carl Schmitt." *Executive Intelligence Review* 33.1 (Jan. 2006), www.larouchepub.com/other/2006/3301c_schmitt_profile.html; Jerome Eric Copulsky, "King of Pain: The Political Theologies of '24,'" *Sightings* (March 1, 2007). marty-center.uchicago.edu/sightings/archive_2007/0301.shtml (accessed 6/19/2007).

34. Cf. G. W. Bush, Address to UN Assembly (Sept. 23, 2003), www.whitehouse.gov/news/releases/2003/09/20030923-4.html.

35. G. W. Bush, Address to UN Assembly.

36. Cf. www.whitehouse.gov/news/releases/2005/01/20050120-1.html.

37. Cf. www.whitehouse.gov/news/releases/2005/01/20050120-1.html.

38. Cf. "The National Security Strategy of the United States of America" (September, 2002), www.whitehouse.gov/nsc/nss.html.

39. Paul Virilio documents the long history of technologically mediated images of conflict, or what he calls the "logistics of military perception" in his *War and Cinema*, trans. Patrick Camiller (New York: Verso, 1989).

40. On the GIG, see www.nsa.gov/ia/industry/gigscope.cfm. See also Jean Baudrillard, *Simulations*, trans. Paul Foss, Paul Patton, and Philip Beitchman (New York: Semiotext(e), 1983).

41. For further discussion of possible connections, see William Connolly, "The Evangelical-Capitalist Resonance Machine," *Political Theory* 33.6 (2005): 869–86; Wendy Brown, "Neo-liberalism and the End of Liberal Democracy," *Theory & Event* 7.1 (2003).

42. Cf. Edward Wong, "Iraq's Curse: A Thirst for Final, Crushing Victory." *New York Times Online*, June 3, 2007, op-ed.

43. Wong, "Iraq's Curse."

44. Cf. Hardt and Negri, *Multitude*, 20, 277.

45. Walter Laqueur, "The Terrorism to Come." *Policy Review* (Aug./Sept. 2004), www.hoover.org/publications/policyreview/3437231.html.

46. Cf. Müller, *A Dangerous Mind*, 39: "As [Schmitt] was only to recognize much later, National Socialism accelerated the fateful modern developments he deplored, rather than provide a model of political action to restrain them."

47. "Donald Rumsfeld 'in his own words,' Excerpts from Sept. 3 Interview on the Events Following the September Attacks." *New York Times*, Sept. 4, 2002, A10.

48. Cf. United States Department of Defense, News Transcript, Presenter: Secretary of Defense Donald H. Rumsfeld (January 22, 2003), www.defenselink.mil/news/Jan2003/t01232003_t0122sdfpc.html.

49. Cf. "Secretary Rumsfeld Interview with CBS Face the Nation," November 11, 2001, www.defenselink.mil/transcripts/transcript.aspx?transcriptid=2368.

50. "Secretary Rumsfeld Interview with CBS Face the Nation."

51. Cf. Carl Schmitt, *The Crisis of Parliamentary Democracy*, trans. Ellen Kennedy (Cambridge, MA: MIT Press, 1988), 75.

52. David Brooks, "The Osama Litmus Test," *New York Times*, Oct. 30, 2004, A31, op-ed.

53. Brooks, "The Osama Litmus Test."

54. Stanley J. Tambiah, *Leveling Crowds* (Berkeley: University of California Press, 1996), 81.

55. Carl Schmitt, *Partisan*, 43. It should be emphasized that for Clausewitz, the distinction between high and low does not correspond to that between emotion and reason. Rather, it concerns the complexity and breadth of emotional operations. Cf. Clausewitz, *On War*, 139.

56. Cf. *Legaliät und Legitimität*, Carl Schmitt (Munchen: Duncker & Humblot, 1932).

57. Antulio J. Echevarria, II, "Clausewitz's Center of Gravity: Changing Our Warfighting Doctrine—Again!," September 2002, www.clausewitz.com/CWZHOME/ECHEVAR/gravity.pdf.

58. Echevarria, "Clausewitz's Center of Gravity."

59. Cf. John McCain, "Meet the Press," MSNBC, Aug. 20, 2006, www.msnbc.msn.com/id/14390980/.

60. On Schmitt and Morgenthau, see William Scheuerman, "Carl Schmitt and Hans Morgenthau: Realism and Beyond," in *Reconsidering Realism: The Legacy of Hans J. Morgenthau*, ed. Michael Williams (Oxford: Oxford University Press, 2007).

61. Zbigniew Brzezinski, "A Must-Read Speech: Zbigniew Brzezinski's Remarks from the 'New American Strategies for Security and Peace' Conference," *The American Prospect Online*, October 31, 2003. www.prospect.org/cs/articles?article=a_mustread_speech.

62. C. Friedrich and Z. Brzezinski, *Totalitarian Dictatorship and Autocracy* (New York: Praeger Publishers, 1965), 202.

63. Zbigniew Brzezinski, "How to Make New Enemies," *New York Times*, October 25, 2004, A25, op-ed.

64. Brzezinski, "How to Make New Enemies."

65. Brzezinski, "How to Make New Enemies."

66. Cf. "Zbigniew Brzezinski: 'Tactician for the Establishment,'" *MERIP Reports* 54 (Feb. 1977): 18–19; Robert Kuttner, "A Conversation with Zbigniew Brzezinski," May 23, 2007, www.miftah.org.

67. Adam Nagourney and Elisabeth Bumiller, "Bush Takes on Direct Role in Shaping Election Tactics," *New York Times*, August 29, 2004, A18.

68. Cf. Laqueur, "The Terrorism to Come." Compare Paul Krugman, "Snares and Delusions," *New York Times*, April 13, 2004, A27, op-ed: "Again and again, administration officials have insisted that some particular evildoer is causing all our problems. . . . The obvious point that we're facing widespread religious and nationalist resentment in Iraq, which is exploited but not caused by the bad guy *du jour*, never seems to sink in."

69. Crawford Young, *The Politics of Cultural Pluralism* (Madison: University of Wisconsin Press, 1976), 5.

70. Schmitt, *Partisan*, 69.

71. Carl Schmitt, *The Crisis of Parliamentary Democracy*, 71.

72. Cf. Simona Draghici, "Foreword" to Schmitt, *Land and Sea*, ix.

73. Schmitt, *Partisan*, 23.

~

Bibliography

Carl Schmitt in English Translation

Schmitt, Carl. *Appropriation/Distribution/Production: An Attempt to Determine from Nomos the Basic Questions of Every Social and Economic Order*, appendix to Schmitt, *The Nomos of the Earth*.

——. *The Concept of the Political*. Translated by George Schwab (New Brunswick, NJ: Rutgers University Press, 1976).

——. *The Crisis of Parliamentary Democracy*. Translated by Ellen Kennedy. Cambridge, MA: MIT Press, 1988.

——. *Four Articles*. Translated by Simona Draghici. Corvallis, OR: Plutarch Press, 1999.

——. *Land and Sea*. Translated by Simona Draghici. Corvallis, OR: Plutarch Press, 1997.

——. *Legality and Legitimacy*. Translated and edited by Jeffrey Seitzer. Durham, NC: Duke University Press, 2004.

——. *The Nomos of the Earth*. Translated by G. L. Ulmen. New York: Telos, 2003.

——. *Political Theology*. Translated by George Schwab. Chicago: MIT Press, 1988.

——. *Political Romanticism*. Translated by Guy Oakes. Cambridge, MA: MIT Press, 1986.

——. *Roman Catholicism and Political Form*. Translated by G. L. Ulmen. Westport, CT: Greenwood Press, 1996.

——. *Theory of the Partisan*. Translated by G. L. Ulmen. *Telos* 127 (Spring 2004): 11–78.

——. *The Visibility of the Church*. Translated by G. L. Ulmen, appendix to Schmitt, *Roman Catholicism and Political Form*.

———. *War/Non-War, A Dilemma*. Translated by Simona Draghici. Corvallis, OR: Plutarch Press, 2004.

Carl Schmitt in German

Schmitt-Doroti, Carl. *Die Diktatur*. München: Duncker & Humblot, 1921.

Schmitt, Carl. *Der Begriff des Politischen*. Berlin: Duncker & Humblot, 2002.

———. *Der Nomos der Erde im Volkerrecht des Jus Publicum Europaeum*. Berlin: Duncker & Humblot, 1997.

———. *Die geistesgeschichtliche Lage des heutigen Parlamentarismus*. München und Leipzig: Duncker & Humblot, 1926.

———. *Legaliät und Legitimität*. München und Leipzig: Duncker & Humblot, 1932.

———. *Politische Romantik*. Berlin: Duncker & Humblot, 1919.

———. *Römischer Catholizismus und politische Form*. Stuttgart: Klett-Cotta, 1984.

———. *Theorie des Partisanen*. Berlin: Duncker & Humblot, 2002.

———. *Verfassungslehre*. München und Leipzig: Duncker & Humblot, 1928.

Other Sources

Agamben, Giorgio. *Homo Sacer*. Stanford: Stanford University Press, 1998.

Anderson, Benedict. *Imagined Communities*. New York: Verso, 1991.

Appadurai, Arjun. *Modernity at Large*. Minneapolis: University of Minnesota Press, 1996.

Arendt, Hannah. *The Origins of Totalitarianism*. San Diego: Harcourt, 1976.

———. *The Human Condition*. Chicago: University of Chicago Press, 1958.

Attell, Kevin, trans. *State of Exception*. Chicago: University of Chicago Press, 2005.

Balakrishnan, Gopal. *The Enemy*. New York: Verso, 2000.

Barber, Benjamin. *Jihad vs. McWorld*. New York: Times Books, 1995.

Baudrillard, Jean. *Simulations*. Translated by Paul Foss, Paul Patton, and Philip Beitchman. New York: Semiotext(e), 1983.

Bendersky, Joseph W. "Carl Schmitt and the Conservative Revolution." *Telos* 72 (Summer 1987): 27–42.

———. "Carl Schmitt at Nuremberg." *Telos* 72 (Summer 1987): 91–129.

———. *Carl Schmitt: Theorist for the Reich*. Princeton, NJ: Princeton University Press, 1983.

Benjamin, Walter. "The Work of Art in the Age of Its Mechanical Reproducibility." In *Walter Benjamin: Selected Writings*, edited by Howard Eiland and Michael W. Jennings, vol. 4. Cambridge, MA: Harvard University Press, 2003.

Blumenberg, Hans. *The Legitimacy of the Modern Age*. Cambridge, MA: MIT Press, 1983.

Brown, Wendy. "Neo-liberalism and the End of Liberal Democracy." *Theory & Event* 7.1 (2003).

Brunner, Otto. *Land and Lordship*. Translated by Howard Kaminsky and James Van Horn Melton. Philadelphia: University of Pennsylvania Press, 1992.

Carr, E. H. *The Twenty Years' Crisis*. New York: Harper & Row, 1964.

Cassirer, Ernst. *The Individual and the Cosmos*. Translated by Mario Domandi. New York: Dover (2000).

Castells, Manuel. "Global Governance and Global Politics." *Political Science and Politics* 38.1 (Jan. 2005): 9–16.

Clausewitz, Carl Von. *On War*. Translated by Michael Howard and Peter Paret. Princeton, NJ: Princeton University Press, 1984.

Cohen, Roger. "What's in It for America." *New York Times*, March 6, 2005, Week in Review section, p. 1.

Colliot-Thélene, Catherine. "Carl Schmitt versus Max Weber." In *The Challenge of Carl Schmitt*, edited by Chantal Mouffe. New York: Verso, 1999.

Connolly, William E. "The Complexity of Sovereignty," in *Sovereign Lives: Power in Global Politics*, edited by Jenny Edkins, Véronique Pin-Fat, and Michael J. Shapiro. New York: Routledge, 2004.

———. "The Evangelical-Capitalist Resonance Machine." *Political Theory* 33.6 (2005).

———. *Pluralism*. Durham, NC: Duke University Press, 2005.

Cristi, Renato. *Carl Schmitt and Authoritarian Liberalism*. Cardiff, UK: University of Wales Press, 1998.

Dahl, Robert. "The Myth of the Presidential Mandate." *Political Science Quarterly* 105 (Autumn 1990): 355–72.

de Certeau, Michel. *The Politics of Everyday Life*. Berkeley: University of California Press, 2002.

Deleuze, Gilles, and Felix Guattari. *A Thousand Plateaus*. Minneapolis: University of Minnesota Press, 1987.

deMan, Paul. "Pascal's Allegory of Persuasion." In *Allegory and Representation*, edited by Stephen Greenblatt. Baltimore, MD: Johns Hopkins University Press, 1981.

Derrida, Jacques. "Force of Law: The Mystical Foundation of Authority." In *Deconstruction and the Possibility of Justice*, edited by Drucilla Cornell. New York: Routledge, 1992.

———. "Passions." In *Derrida: A Critical Reader*, edited by David Wood. Cambridge, UK: Blackwell, 1992.

———. *The Politics of Friendship*. New York: Verso, 1997.

Dyzenhaus, David, ed. *Law as Politics*. Durham, NC: Duke University Press, 1998.

Echevarria, Antulio J., II. "Clausewitz's Center of Gravity: Changing Our Warfighting Doctrine—Again!" www.clausewitz.com/CWZHOME/ECHEVAR/gravity.pdf.

Friedrich, Carl, and Zbigniew Brzezinski. *Totalitarian Dictatorship and Autocracy*. New York: Praeger Publishers, 1965.

Fynsk, Christopher. "A Nomos without Truth." *South Atlantic Quarterly* 104.2 (Spring 2005): 313–17.

Gasché, Rodolphe. "The Partisan and the Philosopher." *South Atlantic Quarterly* 104.2 (Spring 2005): 9–34.

Gerth, H. H., and C. Wright Mills, eds. *From Max Weber*. New York: Oxford University Press, 1946.

Gross, Raphael. *Carl Schmitt and the Jews*. Translated by Joel Golb. Madison: University of Wisconsin Press, 2007.

Habermas, Jurgen. *Legitimation Crisis*. Boston: Beacon Press, 1975.

———. *The Structural Transformation of the Public Sphere*. Cambridge, MA: MIT Press, 1991.

Hardt, Michael, and Antonio Negri. *Empire*. Cambridge, MA: Harvard University Press, 2000.

———. *Multitude*. New York: Penguin, 2004.

Hardt, Michael, and Thomas Dumm. "Sovereignty, Multitudes, Absolute Democracy: A Discussion between Michael Hardt and Thomas Dumm about Hardt and Negri's Empire." *Theory and Event* 4 (3), par. 23, 2000.

Hegel, G. W. F. *Philosophy of Right*. Translated by T. M. Knox. New York: Oxford University Press, 1952.

Hewitt, Andrew. *Fascist Modernism*. Stanford, CA: Stanford University Press, 1993.

Hobbes, Thomas. *Leviathan*. Oxford: Oxford University Press, 1998.

Hobsbawm, Eric. *The Age of Extremes*. New York: Vintage Books, 1996.

Hopkins, Jasper. *Nicholas of Cusa on Learned Ignorance: A Translation and an Appraisal of* De Docta Ignorantia. Minneapolis, MN: Banning Press, 1985.

Horkheimer, Max. "Changes in the Structure of Political Compromise." In *The Essential Frankfurt School Reader*. New York: Continuum, 1982.

Huntington, Samuel P. "The Clash of Civilizations?" *Foreign Affairs* 72 (Summer 1993): 22–49.

Jameson, Frederic. "Notes on Nomos." *South Atlantic Quarterly* 104.2 (Spring 2005): 199–204.

Kantorowitz, Ernst H. *The King's Two Bodies: A Study in Medieval Political Theology*. Princeton, NJ: Princeton University Press, 1957.

Kellner, Douglas. "Presidential Politics: The Movie." *American Behavioral Scientist* 46.4 (2002): 467–86.

Kelly, Duncan. "Carl Schmitt's Political Theory of Representation." *Journal of the History of Ideas* 65.1 (2004): 113–34.

Kennedy, Ellen. *Constitutional Failure, Carl Schmitt in Weimar*. Durham, NC: Duke University Press, 2004.

Kracauer, Sigfried. *From Caligari to Hitler*. Princeton, NJ: Princeton University Press, 2004.

Lenin, V. I. *What Is to Be Done*. New York: International Publishers, 1969.

Machiavelli, Niccolò. *Selected Political Writings*. Edited by David Wooton. Indianapolis, IN: Hackett, 1994.

Marx, Karl. "Contribution to the Critique of Hegel's Philosophy of Right: Introduction." In *The Marx-Engels Reader*, edited by Robert C. Tucker. New York: Norton, 1978.

Massumi, Brian. *Parables for the Virtual*. Durham, NC: Duke University Press, 2002.

McCormick, John P. *Carl Schmitt's Critique of Liberalism*. Cambridge, UK: Cambridge University Press, 1997.

Meier, Heinrich. *The Lesson of Carl Schmitt*. Chicago: University of Chicago Press, 1998.

Michaud, Eric. *Un Art De L'Éternité*. Paris: Gallimard, 1996.

Mouffe, Chantal, ed. *The Challenge of Carl Schmitt*. New York. Verso, 1999.

Mouffe, Chantal. *The Democratic Paradox*. New York: Verso, 2000.

———. *The Return of the Political*. New York: Verso, 1993.

Mosse, George. *Masses and Man*. New York: Howard Fertig, 1980.

Müller, Jan-Werner. *A Dangerous Mind*. New Haven, CT: Yale University Press, 2003.

Mussolini, Benito. *Fascism, Doctrine and Institutions*. New York: Howard Fertig, 1968.

Neumann, Franz. *Behemoth*. New York: Harper & Row, 1944.

Nicholas of Cusa. *The Vision of God*. Translated by Emma Gurney Salter. New York: Frederick Unger Publishing Co., 1960.

Paxton, George. *The Anatomy of Fascism*. New York: Vintage Books, 2005.

Piccone, Paul, and G. L. Ulmen. "Introduction to Carl Schmitt." *Telos* 72 (Summer 1987): 3–14.

Polanyi, Karl. *The Great Transformation*. Boston: Beacon Press, 2001.

Rahner, Karl, and Herbert Vorgrimler. *Theological Dictionary*. Edited by Cornelius Ernst. Translated by Richard Strachan. New York: Herder and Herder, 1965.

Rousseau, Jean-Jacques. *On the Social Contract*. Translated by Judith Masters. New York: St. Martin's Press, 1978.

Scheuerman, William. *Carl Schmitt*. Oxford: Rowman & Littlefield, 1999.

———. "Carl Schmitt and Hans Morgenthau: Realism and Beyond." *Reconsidering Realism: The Legacy of Hans J. Morgenthau*. Edited by Michael Williams. Oxford: Oxford University Press, 2007.

———. *Liberal Democracy and the Social Acceleration of Time*. Baltimore, MD: Johns Hopkins University Press, 2004.

Schnapp, Jeffrey. *Staging Fascism*. Stanford, CA: Stanford University Press, 1996.

Schumpeter, Joseph. *Capitalism, Socialism and Democracy*. New York: Harper Perennial, 1976.

Schwab, George. *The Challenge of the Exception*. Berlin: Dunker & Humblot, 1970.

Shapiro, Kam. "The Myth of the Multitude." In *The Empire's New Clothes*. New York: Routledge, 2003.

———. *Sovereign Nations, Carnal States*. Ithaca, NY: Cornell University Press, 2003.

———. "Sovereignty, Multitudes, Absolute Democracy: A Discussion between Michael Hardt and Thomas Dumm about Hardt and Negri's Empire." *Theory and Event* 4.3.

Tambiah, Stanley J. *Leveling Crowds*. Berkeley: University of California Press, 1996.

Taubes, Jacob. *The Political Theology of Paul*. Translated by Dana Hollander. Stanford, CA: Stanford University Press, 2004.

Thornhill, Chris. *Political Theory in Modern Germany*. Cambridge, UK: Polity Press, 1999.

Virilio, Paul. *Speed and Politics*. Translated by Mark Polizzotti. New York: Semiotext(e), 1986.

———. *War and Cinema*. Translated by Patrick Camiller. New York: Verso, 1989.

Virilio, Paul, and Sylvere Lotringer. *Pure War*. New York: Semiotext(e), 1983.

Weber, Max. *Economy and Society*. Berkeley: University of California Press, 1978.

Wolfe, Alan. "A Fascist Philosopher Helps Us Understand Contemporary Politics." *The Chronicle of Higher Education* 50.30: B16, 2004.

Wolin, Richard. "Carl Schmitt: The Conservative Revolutionary Habitus and the Aesthetics of Horror." *Political Theory* 20 (1992): 424–47.

Zizek, Slavoj. *The Ticklish Subject*. New York: Verso, 1999.

Index

acclamation, Schmitt's discussion of, 7,
    19–20, 48–49, 53, 57, 63n65
Agamben, Giorgio, 8, 10, 36n93, 101–2
Anderson, Benedict, 40
antisemitism, Schmitt's, 7, 13–14n28
Appadurai, Arjun, 104, 110
Arendt, Hannah, 66n126, 91n8.

Balakrishnan, Gopal, xviiin1, 2, 5, 6, 9,
    10, 14n36, 23, 63n47, 93n45, 115
Barber, Benjamin,104–5
Bendersky, Joseph W., xviiin1, 31, 54,
    62n45, 96n142
Benjamin, Walter, viii, xii–xiv, 44,
    58–60, 104
Blumenberg, Hans, 23
Bolsheviks, 3, 18, 37
Brunner, Otto, 72
Bush, George W. and Administration
    of, 104–7, 112–13
Brzezinski, Zbigniew, 112, 113

Carr, E. H., 10
Cassirer, Ernst, 35n81
Castells, Manuel, 117n1

center of gravity, 6, 58: Donald
    Rumsfeld's use of the phrase (See
    Rumsfeld, Donald); intensity,
    108–10
Clausewitz, Carl Von, 42, 82–84, 86,
    111, 119n55
Colliot-Thelene, Catherine, 8
Complexio Oppositorum, 26–31
Connolly, William E., vii, 43, 119n41
constitutional law: executive power
    and, 18, 57; Rousseau's discussion
    of, 24; Schmitt's theory of, 6, 45–54;
    territorial order and, 72, 77; Weimar,
    3–5, 8, 20
Cusa, Nicholas of, 26

de Certeau, Michel, 93n54
decisionism: democratic
    constitutionalism and popular,
    46–48; Schmitt's critique of liberal
    democracy and his, 20–32; Schmitt's
    theory of, xviii, 5–8, 13n20; in
    Schmitt's theory of political
    territory, 69–75; sovereignty and
    existential, 42–44, 90, 54–59, 62n34

Deleuze, Gilles, xii, 61n24, 102, 104
Derrida, Jacques, viii, ix, x, 32, 95n116
dictatorship, 9, 19–20, 24, 28, 32,
    54–55, 99, 106, 115

Echevarria, Antulio J., II, 111

fascism, viii, xii–xiv; Schmitt's writings
    and, 7–10, 57–59
Friedrich, Carl, 112
Fynsk, Christopher, 91n8, 93n52

Gasche, Rodolphe, 83–85, 87, 92n28
Gross, Raphael, 14n28
Grossräum, 11, 67–68, 78, 81, 99
Guattari, Felix, 61n24, 102, 104

Habermas, Jürgen, 34n34, 64n95
Hardt, Michael and Negri, Antonio, 10,
    101–3
Hegel, G. W. F., viii, x, xi, 3, 38, 88;
    Hegelian, 73, 87
Heidegger, Martin,12n1, 75, 91n8,
    93n52
Hitler, Adolf, 7–9, 11, 13n25, 49, 57,
    59, 65n110, 67, 90n3, 91n7, 106
Hobbes, Thomas, 25, 46–48, 59, 71, 72,
    92n23
Horkheimer, Max, 3
Huntington, Samuel P., 98, 99

intensity: the center of gravity and;
    see center of gravity, terrorism
    and, 114–15; global politics and,
    99, 104; previous discussions of,
    viii–xii; myth and, 38; in Schmitt's
    Theory of the Partisan, 82–90;
    sovereignty and, 7, 41–45, 61n12,
    61n22, 61–62n27, 62n38, 75, 98,
    113

Jameson, Frederic, 12n2, 73, 92n42,
    93n55, 95n97

Kantorowitz, Ernst H., 35n82
Katechon, Schmitt's use of the figure of
    the, 5, 28, 70, 81, 91n7
Kellner, Douglas, 65n109
Kelly, Duncan, 46–48
Kennedy, Ellen, xviiin1, 4, 13n19,
    14n28, 31, 45, 47, 61n12, 64n67,
    65n3

liberalism, Schmitt and the current
    crisis of, 1–4; Schmitt's critique of,
    17–24, 41, 46–47; Schmitt's critique
    of global, 67, 97–104; totalitarianism
    and, 112
Lenin, V. I., 4, 39, 82–83, 85, 95n117,
    99

Machiavelli, Niccolò, vii, 69
Marx, Karl, vii, xii, 88: Marxism,
    Schmitt's messianic reading of 37–
    39, 85, 87, 103, 106
Massumi, Brian, 65n119
Maus, Ingeborg, 10
McCormick, John P., 8, 9, 56–58,
    66–132
Monroe Doctrine, 11, 77, 80, 109
Mouffe, Chantal, xii, 12n5, 99–101
Müller, Jan-Werner, xviiin1, 9–10,
    13n28, 31, 91n7, 93n45, 117n16

Nazism: Schmitt and, 2, 8, 13n28,
    14n29, 59, 71, 89, 93n45
Negri, Antonio. See Michael Hardt
Neumann, Franz, 74

Piccone, Paul. See Ulmen, G. L.
Polanyi, Karl, 63n46
positivism: Schmitt's critique of, 5, 7,
    11, 23, 31–32, 36n92, 116; territorial
    order and, 67–68, 70, 76–79

Romanticism, political, 21–23, 27;
    democratic legitimacy and, 57–60

Rousseau, Jean-Jacques, 19, 24–25, 32, 47, 48, 74, 75, 87, 109
Rumsfeld, Donald, 107–114

Scheuerman, William, 8, 10, 61n27, 93n45, 101–2, 120n60
Schwab, George, xviiin1, 6, 13n28, 32, 35n74, 66n126, 75
Sieyes, Abbé, 19, 46–48
Sorel, Georges, viii, xi, 4, 38–40, 110, 115
sovereignty: aesthetic dimensions of, 10, 59–60; Catholic doctrine and, 27; contemporary modes of, 101–4; dictatorial and commissarial, 18–19; general crisis of, 2–4; international politics and the attenuation of, 67–68, 97–98; intensity and: see intensity, legitimacy of, 5–9; presidential, 54–57; representation and, 46–48; Schmitt's critique of global, 71–78, 81; Schmitt's reconstruction of, xvii–xviii; state of exception and, 19–24

Taubes, Jacob, 14n31
technology: determinism of, 88–89; media and, 40, 56; nature and, 27–28; political administration and, 8–9; territorial order and, 75–77, 88; Walter Benjamin's discussion of, xii–xiii; war and, 68, 72, 80–87
Terrisme, 20, 27; Schmitt's nationalism, 40, 44, 61n15
terrorism xiv, 39 in Schmitt's Theory of the Partisan 68, 83; the war on, 98, 101, 104–116
Thornhill, Chris, 8, 59, 61n20

Ulmen, G. L. and Piccone, Paul, 12n1, 13–14n28, 14n43, 15n41, 103

Virilio, Paul, 95n97, 102–4, 119n39

Weber, Max, 3, 9, 23, 27, 32, 35n61, 50, 57, 59, 63n65
Wolin, Richard, 14n37

Žižek, Slavoj, 99

~

About the Author

Kam Shapiro received his Ph.D. in political science from Johns Hopkins University and currently holds the position of associate professor of politics and government at Illinois State University. His work focuses on somatic dimensions of sovereignty and citizenship. He is the author of *Sovereign Nations, Carnal States* (Cornell University Press, 2003).

www.ingramcontent.com/pod-product-compliance
Lightning Source LLC
Chambersburg PA
CBHW021820270326
41932CB00007B/272